CANDLESTICK CHARTS
Indispensable tool for stock exchange trading

Introduction & First Steps Guide

Siegfried R. Becker

... many THANKS to ISKIA DIANE SALATAN

for her excellent cooperation!

Without her precious assistance,

this book can't be realized.

PREFACE

What drives ordinary citizens to the stock market? Quite simple, it is the desire to safeguard its capital and to increase it at the same time as possible.

Stock market trading is complex and often linguistically even incomprehensible to the layman. Therefore, only after thorough study of exchange trading and its practices, that from a "normal citizen" can become a hopefully successful "stockbroker".

Sufficient market knowledge, strategy and technology are the foundations of a successful speculator.

Trying to explain to the trader of an investment bank or the administrator of an American pension fund the CANDLE STICKS TOPS, would be a scornful unwelcome imposition. Every professional working Trader shows not only in detail the method of Japanese candle analysis, but also perfectly aware that this technique can be an excellent working tool for predicting price movements.

"Can be" - but not must be! Trader and professional stock market investors share almost equal groups into two: Firstly, the daily working with their unqualified supporter of Japanese candlestick charts and; secondly, the equally convinced opponents of this technique.

This book, clear, easy to understand and functional, is aimed primarily to broad users interested in the stock market who wants to develop their own strategies to predict price movements using the graphics of the Japanese candles analysis.

Siegfried R. Becker

CANDLESTICK CHARTS

Indispensable tool
for stock exchange trading

Introduction & First Steps Guide

Published by:
Edition FORMAT 24x36 * 47000 Agen / France

© 2016 Siegfried R. Becker

ISBN 13: 978-2-918933-05-2

TABLE OF CONTENTS

TABLE OF CONTENTS (Continuation)

TABLE OF CONTENTS (Continuation)

PRESENTATION & BOOK CONSTRUCTION

A word about the presentation of the candle combinations in this book:

Looking at the overall picture of candle charts, where you can see with certainty in the previous trading sessions, the different combinations and candle signals that explains them conceded statements easily for right or wrong.

The situation is quite different on which is the last candle to consider, - will it be the candle of the current trading session? or just the last trading day, which hopes to guide the stockbrokers to an investment decision. In order to predict the correct price movement at this moment, only a possible solid knowledge and sufficient practical experience is helpful.

To even the novice or the less experienced stockbrokers to a supportive decision, the individual candles or candle combination are not in the usual alphabetical order or by significance in this book. Your specification depending on the color classification is always made from the LAST in the graphic visible candle.

That is, the reader looks at the last candle and swung his gaze back to the previous candle left it obvious; he sees initially the tendency of the trend to move upward (increase), or downward (decrease).

The color of the last candle (white or black), and the previous trend determines the next chapter.

On the following pages, almost 100 of the most-known candle figures and candle constellations are introduced.

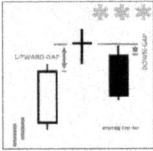

On the respective introduction page of each chapter, the lector will find a summary of each chapter contents in the form of candle miniatures.

Some of these miniatures, as well as the sketch of the candle combinations in the following chapter, are especially marked by stars. These stars indicate the reliability of the signal effect that emanates from the individual figures.

***   3 stars = high reliability of the prediction.
**   2 stars = mediocre reliability.
*   1 star = only limited reliability of prediction.

Candles or candle combinations without stars are to be taken with great caution when considering it.

Generally expressing these assessments by stars, only the opinions and experiences of a relative majority of traders who use daily candlesticks are technical in their predictions.

If this star reflects only the views of a majority of the trader, and not all traders, it must be remembered that the stock market can only function as long as there are two completely opposing opinions. The seller believes to have achieved the best possible price at a given moment, while the buyer is satisfied at the same time when performance is appreciated.

Reviewing the chapter structure:

Reminder: To the possibly inexperienced stock traders to attain a supportive decision, the individual candles or candle combinations are not in the usual alphabetical order or by significance in this book. Your specification depending on the color classification is always made from **the LAST in the graphic visible candle**.

That is, the reader looks at the last candle and swung his gaze back to the previous candle will left it obvious. He initially sees first the tendency of the trend to move upward (INCREASE), or downward, (DECREASE) and then the color of the LAST candle.

Is the LAST candle in a special form? Either striking long or has very short body, with or without upper or lower shadow, etc., ...
Then the reader will first look at **CHAPTER 1**.

If the tendency of an INCREASE is determined (upward), and the last candle is black, the reader will look at **CHAPTER 2.**

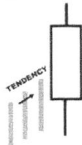

If the tendency of an INCREASE is determined (upward), and the last candle is white, the reader will look at **CHAPTER 3.**

If the tendency of a DECREASE is determined (downward), and the last candle is black, the reader will look at **CHAPTER 4.**

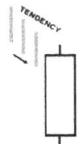

If the tendency of a DECREASE is determined (downward), and the last candle is white, the reader will look at **CHAPTER 5.**

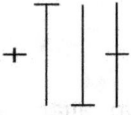

In a trend of INCREASE, (upward), or DECREASE, (downward), and the last candle is a **DOJI**, the reader will look at **CHAPTER 6.**

FIGURES - TABLE OF CONTENTS

(The page number is located inside the figure)

FIGURES - TABLE OF CONTENTS

(The page number is located inside the figure)

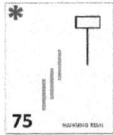

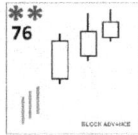

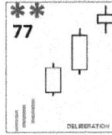

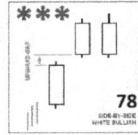

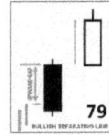

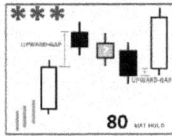

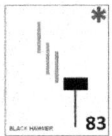

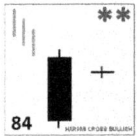

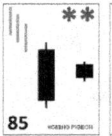

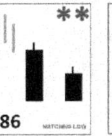

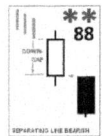

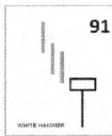

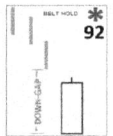

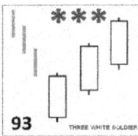

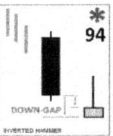

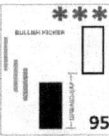

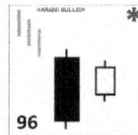

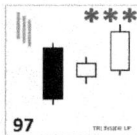

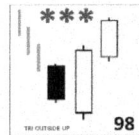

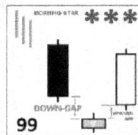

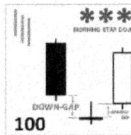

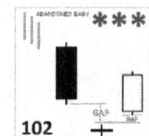

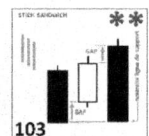

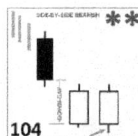

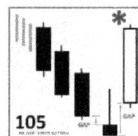

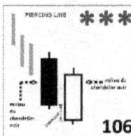

FIGURES - TABLE OF CONTENTS

(The page number is located inside the figure)

15

INTRODUCTION

The various forms of technical analysis

The graphics with curves and lines

The trend thanks to the average share price

The graph of bar charts

Who would dare on the stock exchange even a single order without having been previously informed as thoroughly as possible on the security or its corresponding object value? Stocks, bonds, certificates, etc. ... - no one can seriously imagine placing his money recklessly without analyzing the risk.

There are two methods of analysis to avoid the wrong decisions largely known on the stock exchange: Fundamental analysis and Technical analysis.

Fundamental analysis is based on the general external economic background and knowledge about the publicly quoted securities. That is, if there are shares to be acquired, the use of fundamental analysis includes financial analysis, where all commercial facts and figures as well as the development prospects located behind the public limited company were screened and evaluated. Due to the complexity of fundamental analysis, this is the domain of highly qualified financial experts remains.

Presented by graphics, **technical analysis**, however, is any avid stockbrokers access. It is created solely on the number of performance based and often without any fundamental background and knowledge.

If a part of the "**fundamentalists**", (financial specialists who have, after all, a sound knowledge of the world stock market and its values), doubts the effectiveness of technical analysis, it must be recognized that the majority of working in the stock market as intermediaries and traders will not only order without granting the aid of their technical analysis.

The ideology of the "**technicians**" is the following: The current figures and general data, (data which were so highly rated by the "fundamentalists"), has already been fully integrated at the moment of the quotation from the quoted price. That is once changed, a fundamental economic data or an unexpected business event takes place and when known to the market, the price at this moment adapts instantly.

The "technicians" further say: financial markets have memoirs and independently develop periodic trends. These are triggered by a characteristic on the stock car dynamics without any action of fundamental data.

Various forms of technical analysis

The technical analysis shows in their graphics not only the material present value in paper form but also gives an insight about the sentimental and material thinking and behavior of stockbrokers.

The technical analysis uses in their graphics various techniques and various methods. These are often based on very different market figures and stock market data. The purpose of technical analysis is not in the past. The technical analysis is used for short-term forecasting or long-term trends of future market prices.

The three best-known techniques of market graphs are:

- The display of prices by lines and curves;

- the graphics of Bar Charts;

- the graphics of Japanese Candlesticks

In other graphical analysis, the exchange is closed for most private stockbrokers lacking the necessary internal information, and only professional actors remains accessible.

These are for example:

- MACD, index analysis is very often used;
- RSI analyses the dynamics of the market;
- Bollinger bands;
- analyzing the directional movement;
- the points and characters method;
- the analysis and ETE ETAI;
- the momentum;
- the Ease of Movement;
- the shoulder - head - shoulder method;
- etc.

This list is necessarily incomplete.

LINES AND CURVES

The simplest, but also the most used form of analyzing courses using graphics, is carried out with lines and curves. This type of graphics allows a performance by points, which are interconnected by lines to represent in a certain time period.

Since these graphics do not allow presenting all the information on what is happening within a trading session at the same time, the analyst is forced in the presentation of stock quotes through lines, in making a selection of the criteria. Either he based his analysis on the respective closing prices, the opening prices, the trading session highs, etc...

The possibilities are almost unlimited, but difficult to present together in a single graphic. Probably, most graphics make use of the stock market closing price as a basic instrument. They allow, like other graphics also, the definition of support levels and resistance levels.

As example in this chart: it shows over the course of one year the share price of a listed paper.

The vertical left line is the price scale, the horizontal baseline is the timeline.

The horizontal base line shows the period from January to January +12.

The black zigzag line represents the price development within the period of 12 months. Underlying in

each case of the corresponding trading session are the closing prices. This course line starts, in this example, at a value of 87 in the month of January and ends one year later (January +12), with the value of 119.5.

The line number one, (#1), shows apparently from the price development of cons - standing line. Despite repeated attempts by the market players in the season from January to September to its price, this resistance line in addition, the dynamics of the market forcing the price is always a renewed downturn, a price drop.

The line number two, (#2), however, shows the effectiveness in this period of support line. At no time that the price fell below this line. Also this line is used to lead towards users of the technical, the graphical analysis on the momentum of price moves back.

COURSE AVERAGE LINE

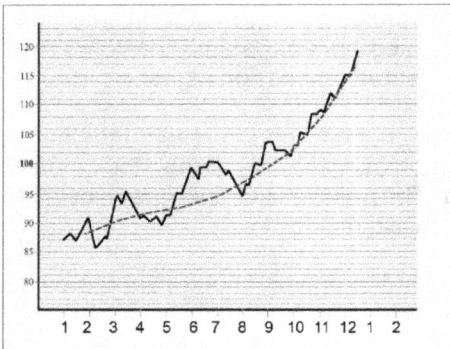

In a line graph, the market trend is represented by a zigzag line.

This line connects the points often far apart, mostly representing the respective trading session close quotes.

This makes the zigzag line formed.

One calculates now the average rate that is, divided to a number of courses by the same number of meetings, and records the result in the graph, the result is a mean value line. Depending on the period, 28, or 200 trading sessions is used as calculating number.

From this average line, it can interpret the evaluation of a listed paper. The real rate is above this average line, the paper is regarded as overvalued. The real rate is below this average line, the paper is considered undervalued.

This shows potential purchase or sale moments.

BAR CHARTS

The Bar Chart uses a horizontal line which reflects the price change between the highest price and the lowest price during a trading session.

This vertical bar is professionally called "Range".

The opening price is shown on the left, and the closing price is on the right side of the longitudinal stroke by a small tick.

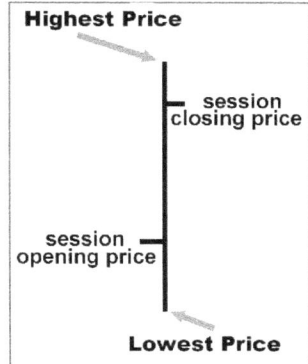

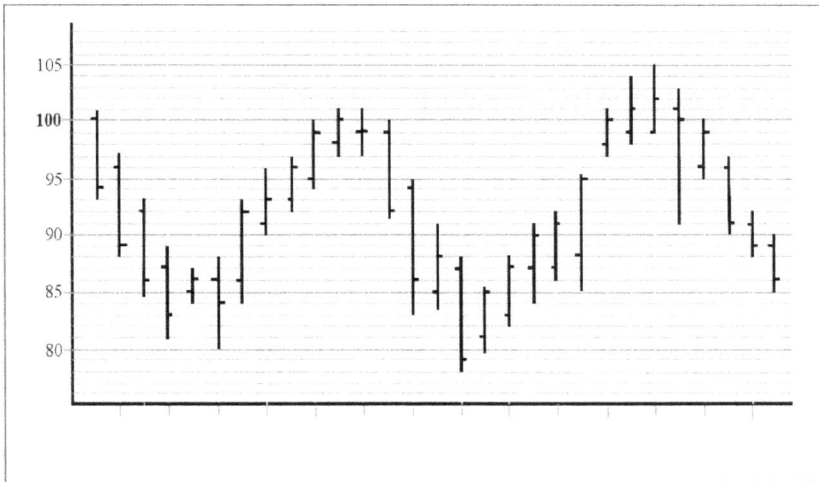

Technical analysis using bar charts is mainly the domain of professional traders. The reading and decoding of bar charts requires sufficient training and experience.

THE CANDLESTICKS

The JAPANESE CANDLESTICKS TECHNIQUE is applied for the first time in the 18th century by a Japanese rice trader, who probably invented it. They say the aid of these candle technology in its rice business; he was able to amass a large fortune.

In circles of bankers, and more and more private investors, the JAPANESE CANDLES TECHNOLOGY enjoys particular popularity.

Both the medium and long-term investment banking, (as well as in day trading), includes CANDLESTICK CHARTS for permanent daily business. No other graphical steering display illuminates the current market sentiment clearly than the CANDLESTICK CHARTS.

If today is engaged in the rapid capital market, thanks to modern computer technology man is ever less and so is the lead entity but is still the man. Be it as programmer for highly complex computer systems or as an active trader. Therefore, the psychological mood and the present act of intention of the investors are indispensable factors of trading exchange. The JAPANESE CANDLESTICKS is ideally suited to represent precisely these factors graphically.

Adding up to this is that the CANDLESTICKS TOPS relatively high success rates as shown at the trend forecast. American studies have shown that, 60-79 percent of previous CANDLESTICKS were right. Compared with other techniques, this is remarkable.

However, these high success rates require a thorough training and preparation for the interpretation of emanating signals from the CANDLESTICKS graphics.

A CANDLESTICK signal can come from both a single, as well as some combination of several candles.

A single candle, such as the HAMMER, can vary depending of previous tendency to express a powerful reversal signal.

Where, however, it must be said that the reliability or trustworthiness of the signal is indeed independent of the number of candles, but when made up of several candles, constellations is usually larger than that of a signal consisting of only a single candle. The fact that the quality of the information brought increased by a multitude of candles, is logical and undeniable.

The Japanese stock market literature uses different candlestick patterns that precedes show either a trend reversal or a continuation of a trend. The two best-known figures are probably the "HAMMER" and "HANGING MAN", two individual candles that are to be interpreted as a sign of an impending trend change. Other very credible formations have names like "MORNINGSTAR", "ENGULFING", "PIERCING LINE" or "THREE WHITE SOLDIERS".

So credible as to also publish some signals, prudent private stockbrokers would never, except in "day trading", be taken pursuant to a single signal, from whatever source it may be, an investment decision. Therefore, so-called evidence should always be taken to help before a position acquisition. One of the most reliable indicators of the notes on the accounts stated "Relative Strength Index", abbreviated as R S I.

Unlike the Bar Charts that convey almost the same information as the candles graphics, the latter are provided with an easy to read additional dimension: the psychological makeup of the market operators. The size of the candle body, small or imposing, and their colors (white, black, red or green), perfectly illustrate the current will of any buyer or seller.

The candles' figure conveys 4 courses of information:

#3 - the opening price;

#2 - the closing price;

#1 - the maximum exchange rate, characterized by a vertical line, called the UPPER SHADOW above the candle body;

#4 - the lowest exchange rate, characterized by a vertical line below the candle body, called LOWER SHADOW.

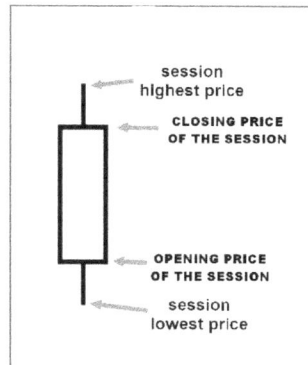
session highest price

CLOSING PRICE OF THE SESSION

OPENING PRICE OF THE SESSION

session lowest price

The position of the opening price and the closing price gives an indication of the trend, bullish or bearish. If tendency is **BULLISH**, it's often figuratively represented by a bull, when running in the trading session in an up mood.

If the opening price is lower than the closing price, so the upward trend is referred to as **BULLISH**. The recorded paper is expensive to trade at the end of trading session than at the opening. The candle is whit but occasionally green.

If tendency is **BEARISH**, it is figuratively represented by a bear, when running in the trading session in a down mood.

#2 - the opening price;
#3 - the closing price;
#1 - the maximum exchange rate, characterized by a vertical line, called the UPPER SHADOW above the candle body;
#4 - the lowest exchange rate, characterized by a vertical line below the candle body, called LOWER SHADOW

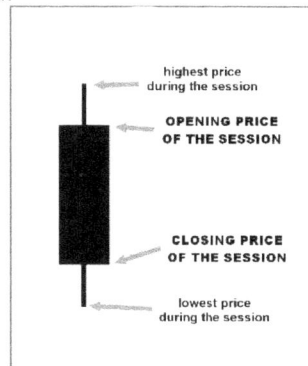
highest price during the session

OPENING PRICE OF THE SESSION

CLOSING PRICE OF THE SESSION

lowest price during the session

If an opening price is higher than the closing price, the downward trend is referred to as **BEARISH**. The trading paper is worth less at end of trading session than at the opening session. The candle is black but occasionally red.

The current mood of the market operators is expressed by the size of the candle body: with the impressive candle body, expectations of market players are greater by significant price changes.

The upper and lower shadows, like the vertical lines above and below the candle body, are also included in this mood barometer.

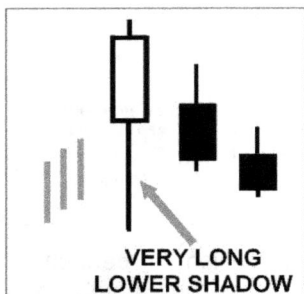

**VERY LONG
LOWER SHADOW**

First example: A very long lower shadow, a vertical long line below the the candle body in an upward trend, expresses the will of the market operators to reduce greatly the course.

Market logic: The current exchange rate is close to a reasonable limit. The stockbrokers benefit. They sell in large quantities and insert the added value obtained. You could draw a new resistance line with this behavior.

**VERY LONG
UPPER SHADOW**

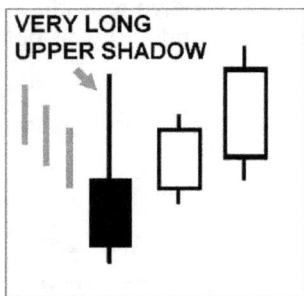

Second example: A very long upper shadow, a vertical long line above the candle body in a downward trend, expresses the will of the market operators to stop the exchange rate drop and may announce a change in trend.

Market logic: Since there is indication that exchange rate is at a very low level to increase the purchase requests. When there's more purchase requests than sales offers, so is the increase of the seller's exchange rate. You could draw in this behavior a new support line.

This will make visible how rich the candles may be. Provided that one knows how to interpret correctly and use correctly this information.

FIRST CHAPTER # 1

CANDLE SIGNALS, which consists of a single figure:

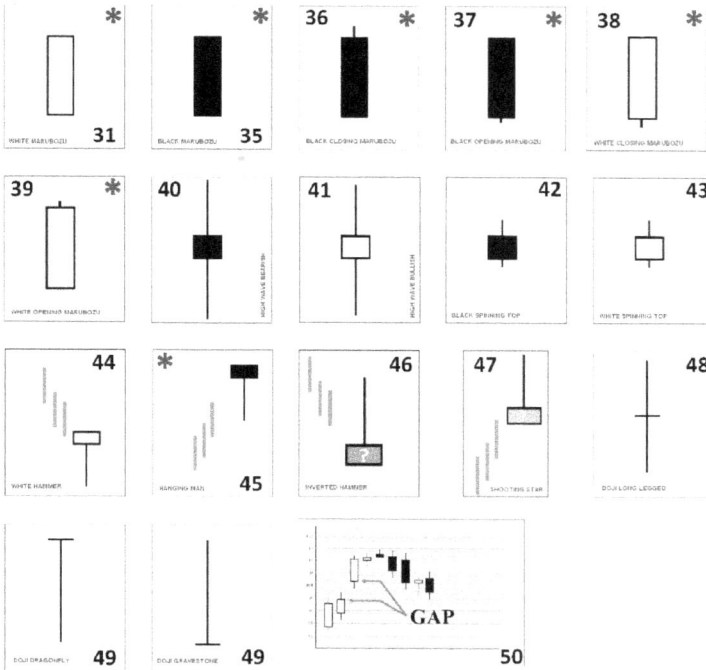

WHITE MARUBOZU **31**	BLACK MARUBOZU **35**	BLACK CLOSING MARUBOZU **36**	BLACK OPENING MARUBOZU **37**	WHITE CLOSING MARUBOZU **38**
WHITE OPENING MARUBOZU **39**	HIGH WAVE BEARISH **40**	HIGH WAVE BULLISH **41**	BLACK SPINNING TOP **42**	WHITE SPINNING TOP **43**
WHITE HAMMER **44**	HANGING MAN **45**	INVERTED HAMMER **46**	SHOOTING STAR **47**	DOJI LONG LEGGED **48**
DOJI DRAGONFLY **49**	DOJI GRAWBSTONE **49**	GAP **50**		

WHITE MARUBOZU

The base figure of the Japanese Candlesticks is the WHITE MARUBOZU, a white block without upper shadow above the block, and without lower shadow below the block.

The opening exchange rate is also the lowest prices in this trading session. During this trading session, the rate rose and closed with the highest exchange rate of this trading session.

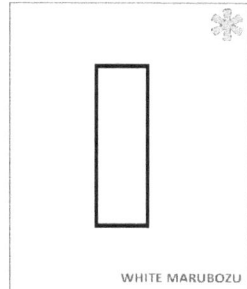

WHITE MARUBOZU

Market logic: To reach such figure, the demand of the buyers must be very strong. This strong demand drives the exchange rate up. The stronger the demand is the higher the exchange rate and therefore the size of the WHITE MAROBUZU. The larger this block, the more attention should cost him. A very powerful WHITE MAROBUZU could announce another price increase for the next three or four trading sessions. Only the short body of the WHITE MAROBUZU is not meaningful.

The WHITE MAROBUZU often arises on the basis of corroborated as well as uncorroborated market rumors and must therefore be viewed with caution.

The Candlesticks analysis can project a support in predicting price movements. However, one should never forget the weaknesses of candles analysis: This analysis is purely technical without involving any unforeseen economic developments. It is based on past price movements and can be instantaneous, where sudden industrial or monetary events are disregarded.

If one look at a candlestick graph after some trading sessions it is relatively simple, the obvious candle combinations reveals their meaning. In deciding moment, by when looking at the LAST candle in a graphic, an assessment of the candle combination is already much more difficult.

WHITE MARUBOZU * Example #1

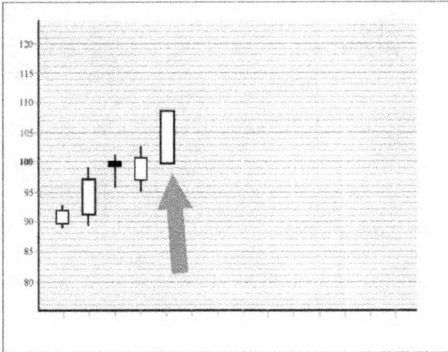

A trading session on the upward trend closes with a significant WHITE MARUBOZU. Is this a signal of continuous upward trend?

Market logic: it is about to takeover a rumor that a competitor want to buy up all securities of this company at "cost what it may be" .

This expects, in principle, an upward rally of the course. This upward movement would have to continue until the interested sellers acquired the desired number of papers.

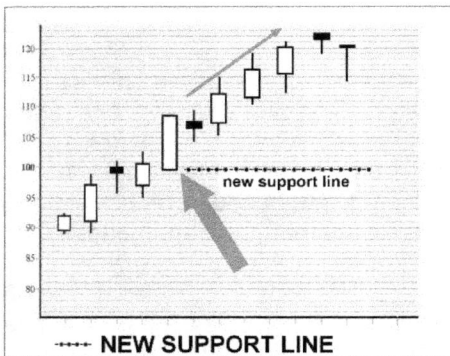

····· NEW SUPPORT LINE

Caused by this takeover rumor the upward trend continues a few trading sessions.

The WHITE MARUBOZU defiance, the courses in the following trading sessions go downhill. A downward trend installs.

Market logic: The rumor has proven to be untrue and the buying speculators abandon their buying positions massively.

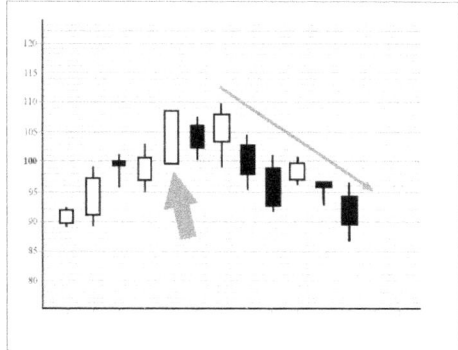

These two examples shows that it is extremely risky to make an investment decision based solely on a single indicator.

If the investor or market players do not have enough time to wait for the following trading sessions and their candle developments, he should induce at least other stock market, such as the PER (Price Earnings Ratio), or sometimes in their own minds, to take advise.

LONG DAYS – SHORT DAYS

Excessive large white or black candles that doesn't have shadows, or just very little upper shadow or lower shadow, are called LONG DAYS. A prerequisite for this name LONG DAY is that the distance between the opening and closing exchange rate is considerable.

Unlike LONG DAYS, short white or black candles are commonly referred to as SHORT DAYS.

A candle can only be referred to as LONG DAY when their body is at least three times greater than the body of the preceding candle.

Market logic: If it appears in a long-term uptrend a WHITE LONG DAY, we may assume that the upward trend continues and a new series of sessions with increasing exchange rates are introduced. This LONG DAY or WHITE MAROBOZU can be the basis of a newly determined support line.

But if it appears in a long-term uptrend a BLACK LONG DAY, this must be assessed as a sign of danger. This BLACK MARUBOZU can signal a tiring of the buyers. Thus it presage a change to the downward trend.

WHITE LONG DAY or BLACK LONG DAY; - cautious market players awaits for the candle configuration of the following trading sessions before they'll take a deciding position.

BLACK MARUBOZU

Compared to the WHITE MARUBOZU the BLACK MARUBOZU has little significance.

BLACK MARUBOZU

The emergence of a WHITE MARUBOZU is only possible if a strong buyer exists, driving the exchange rate upwards.

It is sufficient an inertia, a standstill of the market, to form a BLACK MARUBOZU.

> *Market logic: The BLACK MARUBOZU actually expresses the uncertainty of the market. The sellers have enough papers, but the buyers are much undecided and go preferably in a reticence.*

A BLACK MARUBOZU alone is a very dubious signal.

The BLACK MARUBOZU always requires confirmation in following trading sessions.

Only an overly relative large turnover can transform the feeble signal of the BLACK MARUBOZU into a strong signal.

BLACK CLOSING MARUBOZU

BLACK CLOSING MARUBOZU

The BLACK CLOSING MARUBOZU differs only from BLACK MARUBOZU by the presence of a very short upper shadow above the candle body. This short upper shadow usually arises shortly after the opening of the trading session.

Market logic: For a brief moment, buyers have tried to push the price out above the opening price upwards. But the purchase request was too weak to hold this session in peak price. Thus, the true trend was visibly down of what was exploited immediately with plenty of sellers.

This is a classic warning sign, which often indicates the end of an upward trend.

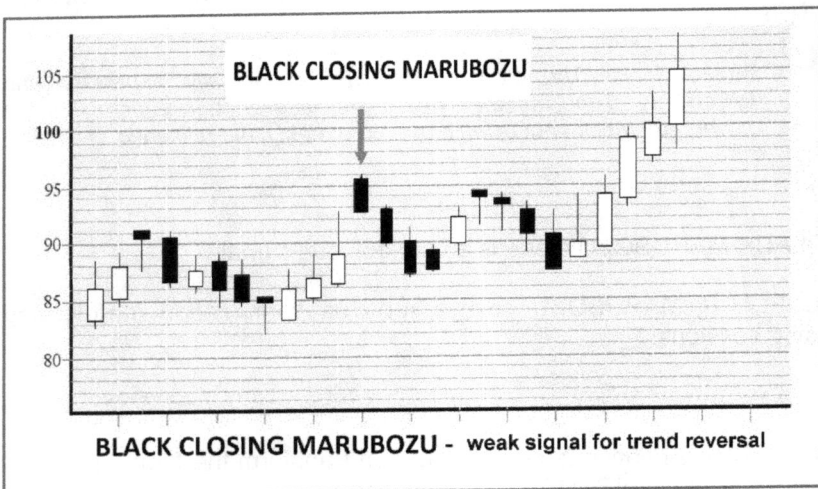

BLACK CLOSING MARUBOZU - weak signal for trend reversal

Like all black candles, the BLACK CLOSING MARUBOZU has only a feeble signal and requires additional evidence to submit comments.

BLACK OPENING MARUBOZU

The BLACK OPENING MARUBOZU differs only from the original BLACK MARUBOZU by the presence of a short lower shadow below the candle body.

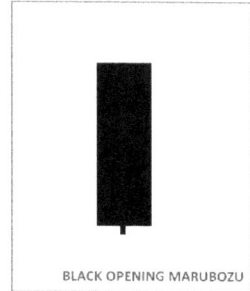

BLACK OPENING MARUBOZU

Market logic: The weak demand from buyers forces the rate to change during the trading session steeply downwards. Only with difficulty that an even lower price could be prevented. The trading session closed but at a price only slightly above the lowest rate of the trading session.

The trend continues: Sales mood

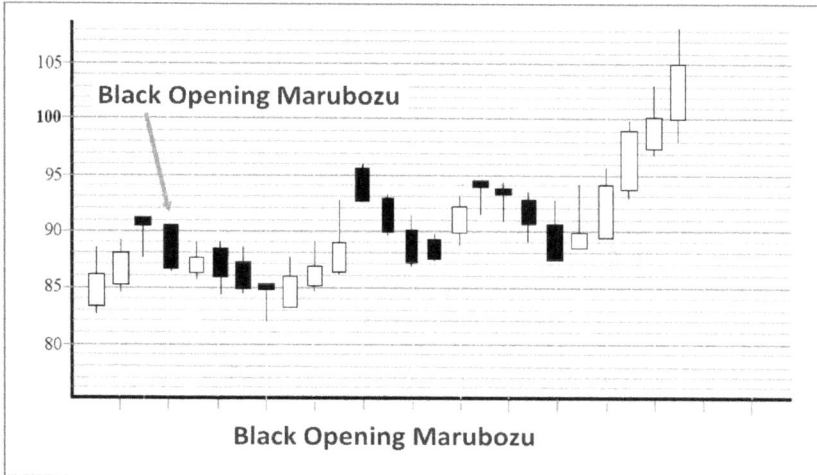

The BLACK OPENING MARUBOZU alone without further evidence allowed no opinion on the further development of the paper.

WHITE CLOSING MARUBOZU

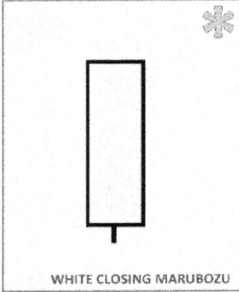

WHITE CLOSING MARUBOZU

The WHITE CLOSING MARUBOZU differs only from the original WHITE MARUBOZU by the presence of a short lower shadow below the candle body.

Market logic: The initially weak demand from buyers forced the price down at first, thus producing a low price which is below the opening price. However, the demand on the part of buyers increased significantly during the trading session. The trading session is closed even with a trading session at a peak exchange rate.

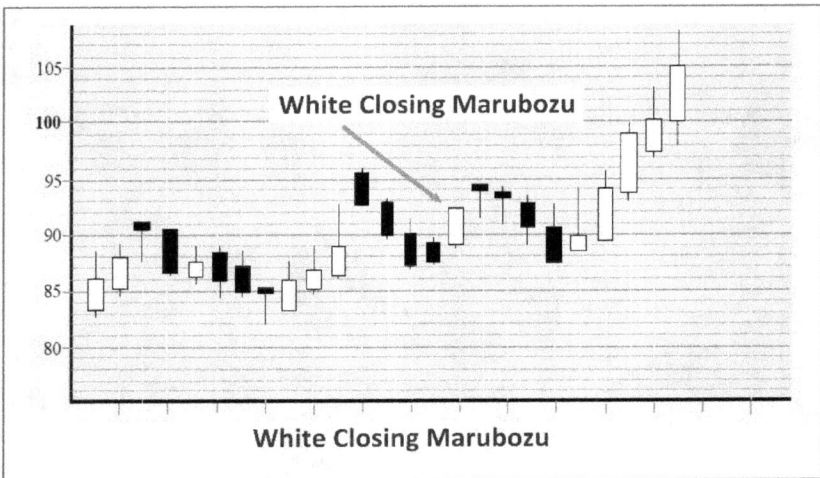

White Closing Marubozu

The signal of the WHITE CLOSING MARUBOZU alone is too weak to decide on a position of acquisition.

WHITE OPENING MARUBOZU

The WHITE OPENING MARUBOZU differs only from the original WHITE MARUBOZU by the presence of a short upper shadow above the candle body.

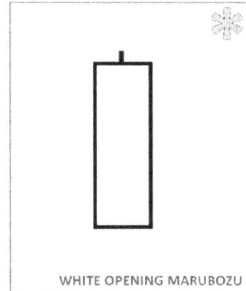

WHITE OPENING MARUBOZU

Market logic: A significant buying demand is driving up the price immediately after the start of trading session. However, the current maximum rate could not be maintained. The trading session closed with a price just below the trading session is the highest rate.

The size of the candle body expresses the strength of the significance of the WHITE OPENING MARUBOZU. Only an imposing body with a very short upper shadow can be considered as a signal.

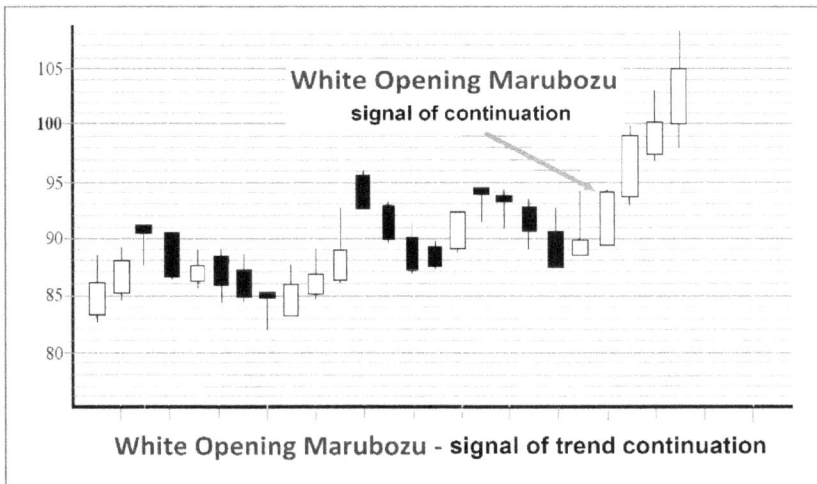

White Opening Marubozu
signal of continuation

White Opening Marubozu - **signal of trend continuation**

No impulsive decision without confirmation by a following white candle or other evidence!

HIGH WAVE BEARISH

BEARISH derived from "bear" = **pessimistic or seller position**;
BULLISH derived from "bull" = **optimistic or buyer position.**

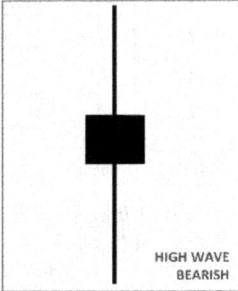

HIGH WAVE
BEARISH

The figure of HIGH WAVE BEARISH, (the pessimistic high wave), consists of a small black candle body and a very long upper shadow plus a very long lower shadow.

Market logic: The HIGH WAVE BEARISH expresses a total indecision of the market operators. There is little difference between the opening price and the closing price. Unsuccessful great efforts on the price change has been made in both upward and downward during the trading session.

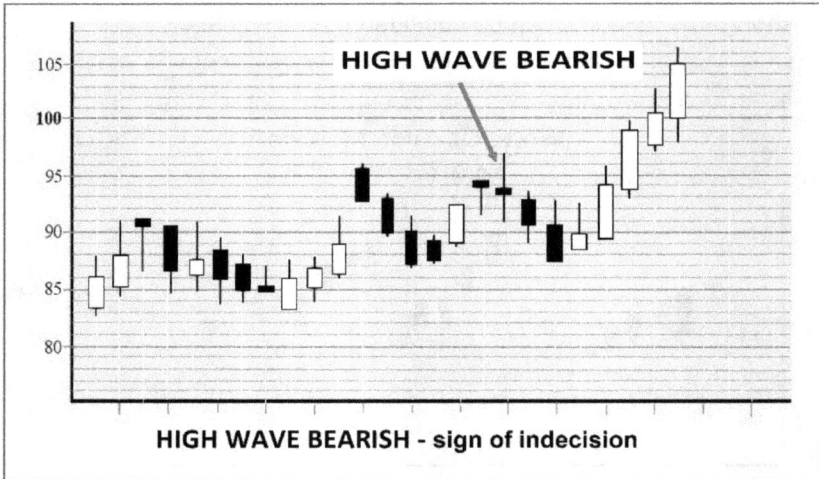

HIGH WAVE BEARISH - sign of indecision

A small candle body and a long upper shadow with a long lower shadow is evidence of a trading session without any special meaning. Only the following trading sessions can provide information on the future trend.

HIGH WAVE BULLISH

BULLISH derived from "bull" **= optimistic or buyer position;**
BEARISH derived from "bear" **= pessimistic or seller position;**

The figure of HIGH WAVE BULLISH, (the optimistic high wave), consists of a small white candle body and a very long upper shadow, as well a very long lower shadow.

The interpretation of HIGH WAVE BEARISH and HIGH WAVE BULLISH are identical.

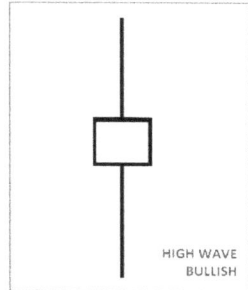

HIGH WAVE
BULLISH

Market logic: The HIGH WAVE BULLISH expresses a total indecision of the market operators. There is little difference between the opening price and the closing price. Unsuccessful great efforts on the price change has been made in both upward and downward during the trading session.

HIGH WAVE BULLISH - **sign of indecision**

Only more indexes can shed light on the future trend.

BLACK SPINNING TOP
or SPINNING TOP BEARISH

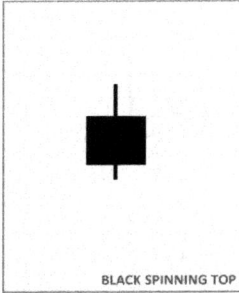

BLACK SPINNING TOP

The figure BLACK SPINNING TOP consists of a small candle body with shadows. The length of the upper or lower shadow doesn't matter unless they form a HIGH WAVE.

Market logic: Feebly market participation and even enthusiasm of both the buyer and the seller. There is indecision about the future rate trend. There is a fragile balance of the market.

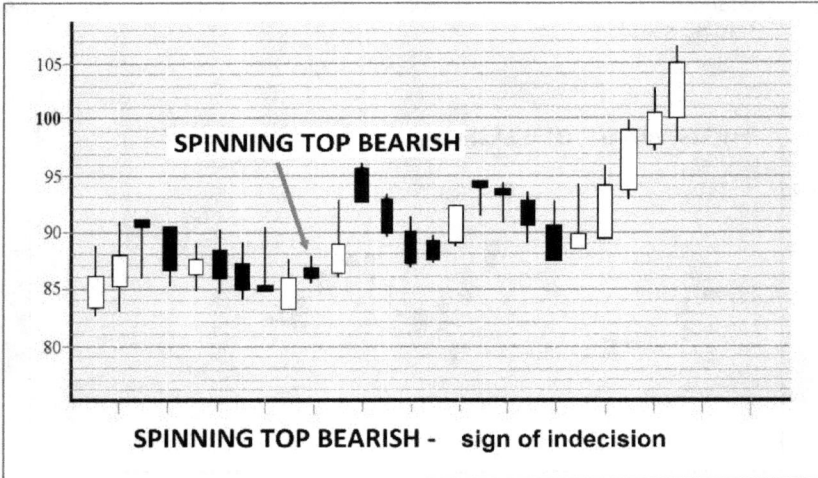

SPINNING TOP BEARISH

SPINNING TOP BEARISH -   sign of indecision

The SPINNING TOP BEARISH is a figure that urges caution: No decision without other indices.

WHITE SPINNING TOP
or SPINNING TOP BULLISH

The figures WHITE SPINNING TOP and BLACK SPINNING TOP are identical.

The figure WHITE SPINNING TOP consists of a small candle body with shadows. The length of the upper or lower shadow doesn't matter as long as they don't transform the figure of HIGH WAVE.

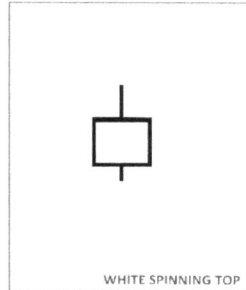

WHITE SPINNING TOP

Market logic: Small market participation and even enthusiasm of both the buyer and the seller. There is indecision about the future exchange rate trend. There is a fragile balance of the market.

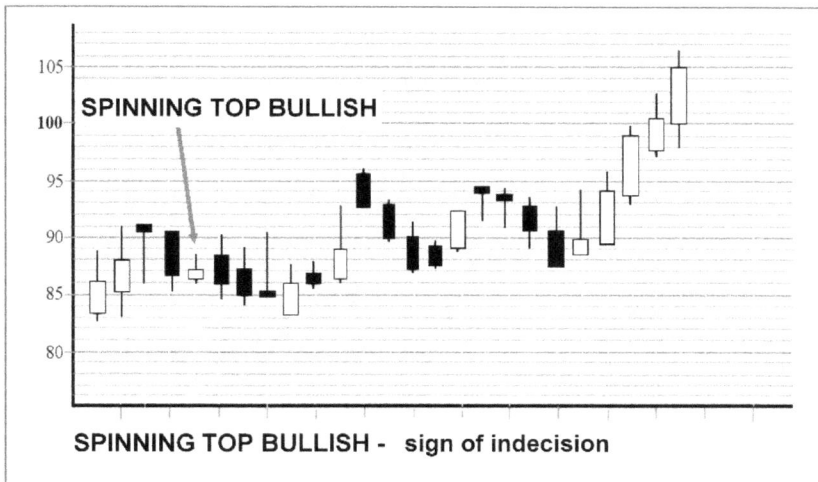

SPINNING TOP BULLISH

SPINNING TOP BULLISH - sign of indecision

The SPINNING TOP BULLISH is a figure that urges caution: No decision without additional indices. □

WHITE HAMMER

The figures WHITE HAMMER and HANGING MAN are identical. They are also probably the most known characters of the candlestick charts.

The WHITE HAMMER announces the end of a downtrend. The HANGING MAN announces the end of an uptrend.

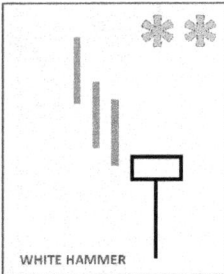

The color of the two figures can be white, as also black.

The WHITE HAMMER consists of a small body with a very long lower shadow. The lower shadow located beneath the body must be at least twice as large as the candles' body.

WHITE HAMMER

The WHITE HAMMER can be a very strong signal of a trend change; especially, if the following candle has a white body.

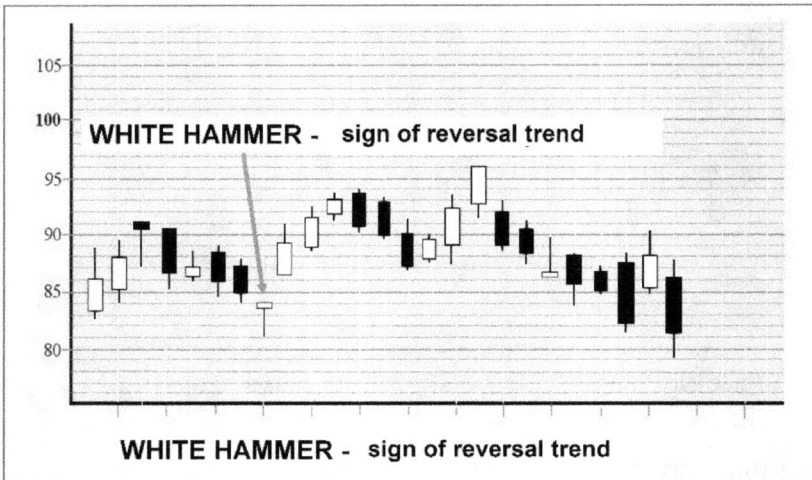

WHITE HAMMER - sign of reversal trend

WHITE HAMMER - sign of reversal trend

BLACK HANGING MAN

The figures HANGING MAN and HAMMER are identical. They are also probably the most known characters of the candle charts.

At the end of an uptrend the figure is called HANGING MAN and at the end of a downtrend is called HAMMER.

The color of the two figures can be white, as also black.

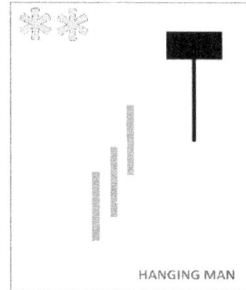

HANGING MAN

The HANGING MAN consists of a small body with a very long lower shadow. The lower shadow located beneath the body must be at least twice as large as the candles' body.

> *Market logic: After a long series on the rise, buyers start to doubt at the height of the course. Immediately after the opening of trading the price falls rapidly in the depth. Frightened by this loss of value, ,the buyer is again in action, thus its price is almost to the level of the opening price. Nevertheless, remained in doubt. These doubts lead a turnaround in all probability.*

The HANGING MAN is a very strong signal of reversal trend. Nevertheless, the next meeting should take confirmation with a big black candle.

HANGING MAN - sign for reversal trend

INVERTED HAMMER

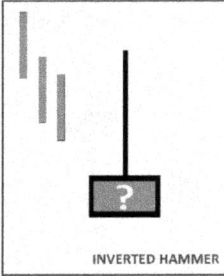

INVERTED HAMMER

According to the title INVERTED HAMMER, this figure represents an upside-down HAMMER.

As the HAMMER is this figure is from a small candle body, but this time with an over-sized upper shadow above the body.

This upper shadow should be at least twice as large as the candle body.

The color of INVERTED HAMMER, black or white, plays a subordinate role.

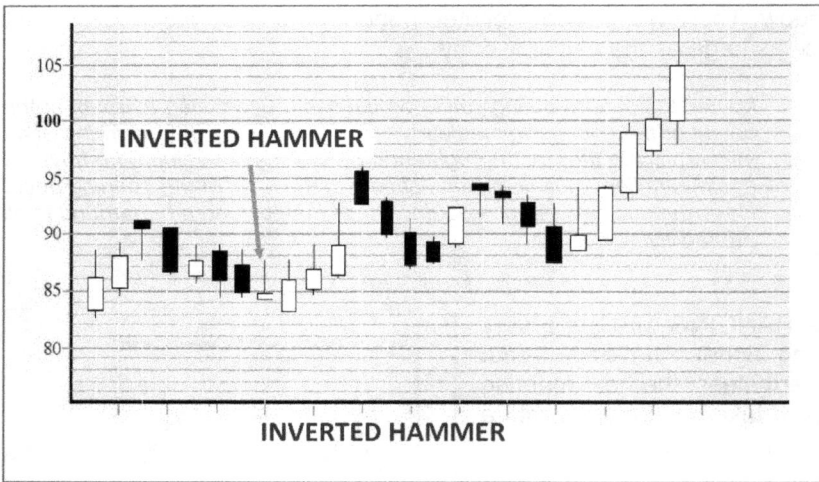

INVERTED HAMMER

The INVERTED HAMMER can announce a reversal trend. However, this signal is a very weak signal. Thus the reliability of this prediction is questionable.

SHOOTING STAR

The figures SHOOTING STAR and INVERTED HAMMER are the same, only the trends, in which they appear, are different. The SHOOTING STAR is formed at the end of an upward trend and can, under certain conditions, expect a reversal of the trend.

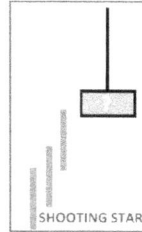

The SHOOTING STAR consists of a small candle body and an over-sized upper shadow above its body.

The significance of this figure, or the possibility of a trend prediction depends largely on the position of SHOOTING STAR within the above previous trends and its representation.

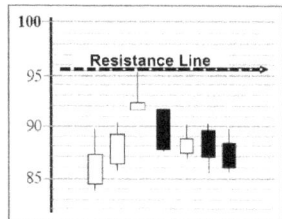

1) At the end of a long series of trading sessions in a constant upward trend, the upper shadow of SHOOTING STAR abuts a resistance line: This is a STRONG signal of reversal trend!

2) Without contact of the upper shadow to an existing resistance line: A reversal trend is possible, but in no case to be regarded as safe.

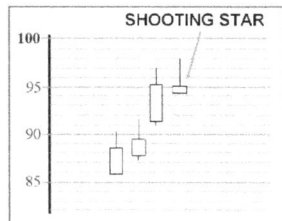

3) Not all of the previous trading sessions consisted of WHITE candles. The SHOOTING STAR is considered to be insignificant.

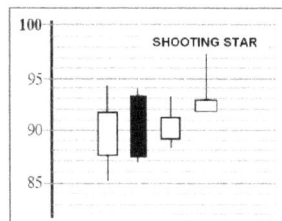

Les DOJI

Are opening and closing rates of a trading session equal, the figure is called DOJI. This is reproduced in the image only by means of a horizontal stroke.

All DOJI's indicate generally the uncertainty of the buyers and sellers.

Market logic: buyers and sellers are in a waiting position. They hope for new information about the market

This hold can still continue in the coming trading sessions and thus produce new DOJI on the graph. Several successions following DOJI can very often involve an upcoming radical reversal of trend. Such brutal trend reversals are often characterized in the graph with the formation of so-called GAP, price jumps without context from. (... see chapter #6)

LONG-LEGGED DOJI

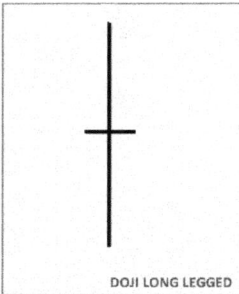

DOJI LONG LEGGED

The LONG-LEGGED DOJI is made of an extremely small candle body, (opening and closing rates are the same), and a very long upper shadow with a very long lower shadow.

Market logic: This figure expresses the extreme uncertainty of the market operators. After biggest rate fluctuations, upwards as well as downwards, the closing rate is swept back to the same height of the opening rate.

Only the coming trading sessions can provide enlightenment.

DOJI DRAGONFLY

Immediately after the opening of the trading session the price crashed. This slump has however been canceled during the trading session and thus closed the seat at the same rate with which it was opened.

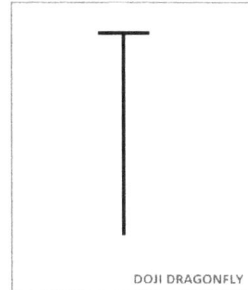

DOJI DRAGONFLY

Market logic: buyer and seller do not know what they want. Only the following trading sessions on the future trend gives information.

DOJI GRAVESTONE

The DOJI GRAVE STONE is the counterpart of the DOJI DRAGONFLY.

Immediately after the opening of trading session the rate climbed enormously. However, this extreme rise collapsed again, so that the trading session is closed at the level of the opening.

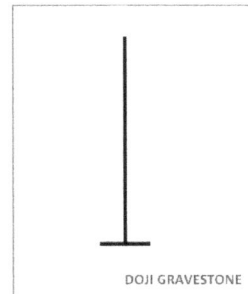

DOJI GRAVESTONE

Should further Doji occur in the following trading sessions, so could this herald a brutal trend change. (... see chapter #6).

GAP

The GAP is not an independent figure. The stockbrokers called it GAP when the resulting window or the price jump and when the opening price of a trading session is not inside the candle body of the previous trading session.

In an uptrend, the opening of the new trading session is higher than the closing price of the previous white candle. Conversely, in a downward trend, the opening price of the new trading session is lower than the closing price of the previous black candle.

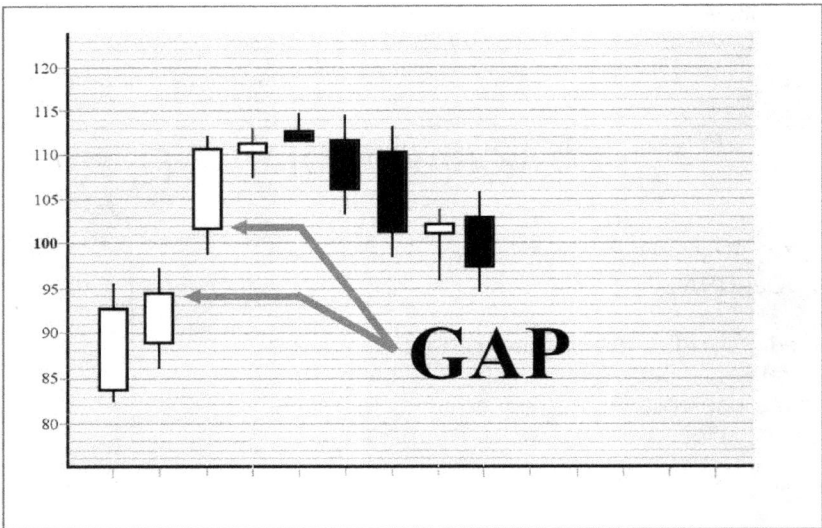

This figure shows an emergence between two white candles GAP: the closing price of the previous white candle is 94; the opening price of the related white candle is 102. Thus, the GAP expresses the price jump 94-102.

The GAP itself should indeed find attention, but does not allow direct conclusion without further indices.

Depending on the position and market trend, and the succeeding candle combinations, GAP is defined follows:

1. ORDINARY GAP, it is of no particular importance and can make any decisions about it. It arises due to minor, insignificant events. This GAP will be closed by the following candle. That is, the price jump will be canceled in the following trading session.

2. The GAP RUNAWAY expresses an acknowledgment of the current price trend. It is connected with a strong sales track and recognizes as such, only if the resulting window is strikingly large.

3. The BREAKAWAY GAP heralds a trend change. It is often accompanied by another significant candle combination. The resulting window will be filled out only in exceptional cases of a following candle. This GAP determines a point of the lead in a downward trend for the emergence of a new support line, or which have an upward trend, the emergence of a newly defined resistance line.

4. The TERMINAL GAP or EXHAUSTION GAP terminates an existing trend. This GAP is but to define safe only after several subsequent trading sessions.

SECOND CHAPTER # 2

TREND: increasing
LAST CANDLE: black

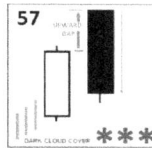

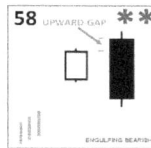

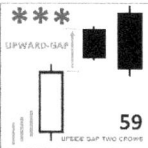

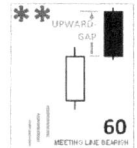

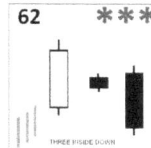

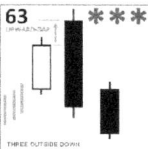

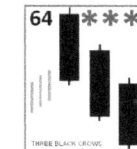

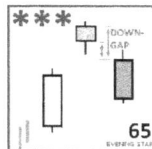

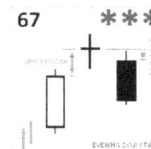

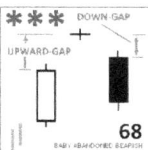

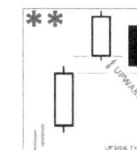

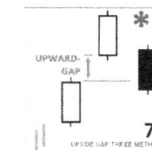

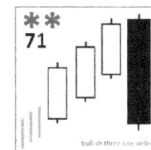

BELT HOLD BEARISH

The BELT HOLD BEARISH may be a signal for a changing trend.

After several sessions in a steady upward trend, a new session with a significant GAP opens.

But instead of continuing the upward trend, the price collapsed during the trading session down to the bottom. The closing price stabilizes very closely to the trading session's lowest price as what is testified to the short lower shadow below the candle body.

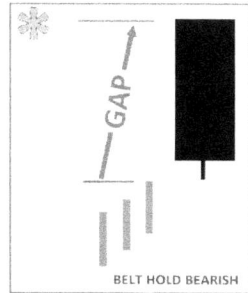

BELT HOLD BEARISH

BELT HOLD BEARISH

BELT HOLD BEARISH - a reversal trend sign- be used with caution

The BELT HOLD BEARISH, a reversal trend sign, but as the sole indication is not confident enough to occupy a position. At least two more trading sessions are required to obtain clarity on the BELT HOLD BEARISH.

BEARISH KICKER

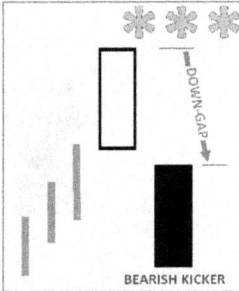

BEARISH KICKER

The BEARISH KICKER consisting of two candles, is a very strong reversal trend sign.

Market logic: This candle combination is often created by unexpected negative information about the stock market listed paper.

Even if the general trend is not important, so you can meet the BEARISH KICKER mostly at the end prolonged upward trends.

Composition:

1) The first to be considered in trading session presents a large white candle without upper shadow and without lower shadow, a WHITE MARUBOZU.

2) The following trading session begins with a significant DOWN GAP (a GAP downwards). Instead, like in the previous trading session to rise, the price falls. He falls at least as much as he rose in the previous trading session and ends as lowest price of the trading session. Thus, this candle is a BLACK MARUBOZU, (black candle without upper shadow and without lower shadow).

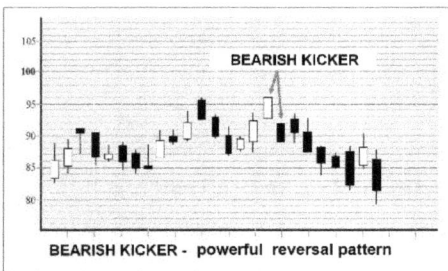

BEARISH KICKER - powerful reversal pattern

This absence of shadows, at the white candle as well as the black candle is very rare and expresses the full force of stockbrokers out to reduce the price.

The BEARISH KICKER is very strong and secure enough signal that heralds a downward trend.

DARK CLOUD COVER

In an uptrend, an especially large white candle can be considered as a reversal trend sign when the next trading session begins with an UPWARD-GAP (upwardly directed window), and their price development is not upward but proceeds downward.

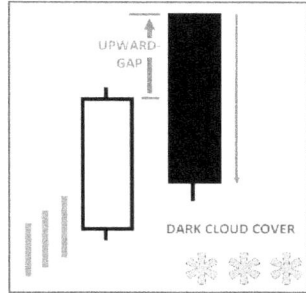

DARK CLOUD COVER

Composition:

1) The UPWARD-GAP is sufficiently large, is important.

2) The second, the black candle loses a large part of the course gained from the previous trading session. The closing price of the black candle should be below half the previous white candle.

Under these conditions, the DARK CLOUD COVER is very strong and sufficiently a reliable signal of reversal trend. It indicates a downward rally, a series of downward trading sessions.

Does the black candle can not manage to fix the closing price below half of the previous white candle, then this "safe" turnaround signals change to a WRONG SIGNAL with the result that the upward trend continues.

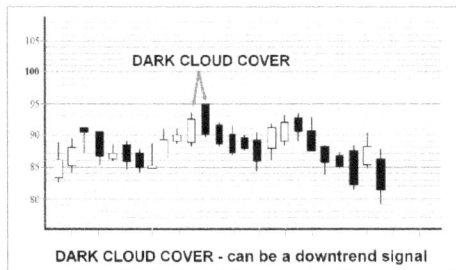

DARK CLOUD COVER - can be a downtrend signal

57

ENGULFING BEARISH

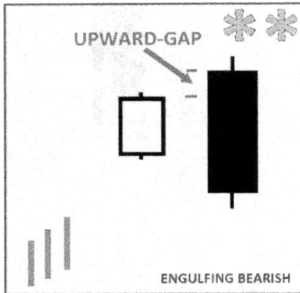

The candle combination of ENGULFING BEARISH is a clear reversal trend sign.

Composition:

1) In an uptrend, it appears a relatively small white candle.

2) The following trading session opened with an UPWARD-GAP (windows upward), and quoted a price crash, going down well over the body shape of the previous white candle.

The Engulfing candle combinations are reliable signals of an impending reversal trend. They quite often occur in the candlestick charts.

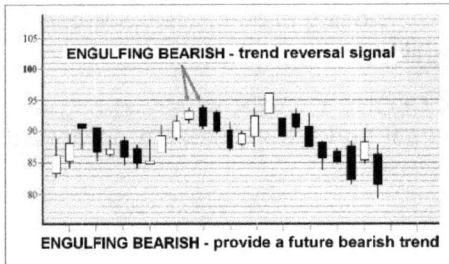

If the black candle reaches to cover the body of the previous candle, (shadow included), this reversal trend signal is reinforced to some.

The height of the black candle plays a role: The greater the candle body the more certain is the signal for reversal trend.

Caution: If this ENGULFING BEARISH is at the end of a downtrend, so it can only be regarded as a reversal trend signal when it clearly breaks through a support line!

UPSIDE GAP TWO CROWS

Even the UPSIDE GAP TWO CROWS is a reversal trend signal.

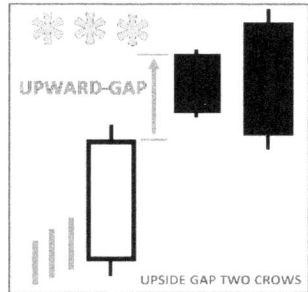

UPWARD-GAP

UPSIDE GAP TWO CROWS

Composition:

1) A large white candle in a constant upward trend.

2) A small black candle appears with a corresponding UPWARD-GAP, (above the white candle opened window).

3) The third trading session shows another black candle whose opening price is above that of the previous trading session and the closing price is below the previous trading session and thus includes the previous black candle completely.

4) The closing price of the last one, the second black candle, still lies above the closing price of the first, the white candle.

The UPSIDE GAP TWO CROWS candle configuration is a strong signal of an impending trend reversal.

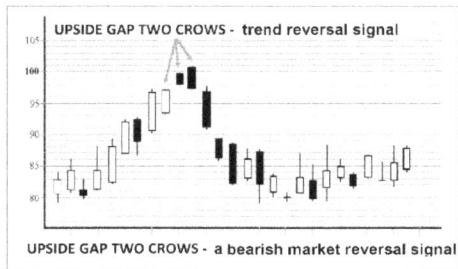

UPSIDE GAP TWO CROWS - trend reversal signal

UPSIDE GAP TWO CROWS - a bearish market reversal signal

MEETING LINE BEARISH

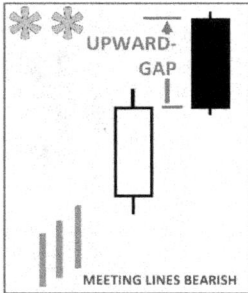

MEETING LINES BEARISH

This candle combination arises in long-term uptrend.

Composition:
1) The first trading session is characterized by a long white candle.

2) The second trading session begins with a very large UPWARD-GAP.

Important: This up window must be at least 60% greater than the white candle body.

3) The closing price of the black candle is exactly or approximately equal to the closing price of the white candle.

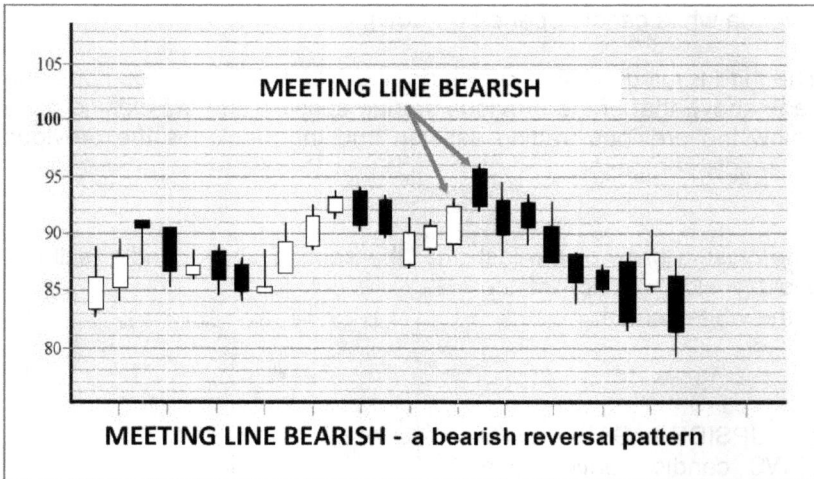

MEETING LINE BEARISH - a bearish reversal pattern

This candle configuration is an inversion signal of the upward trend to a downward trend. Nevertheless, the trader should wait for the confirmation in the next trading sessions, before he takes position.

HARAMI BEARISH

The HARAMI BEARISH occurs mostly at the end of an uptrend.

Market logic: The buyers are doubtful about the high price. Should this candle combination be also followed by another black candle, the buyers dispose this to sellers to get their purchases with slight losses.

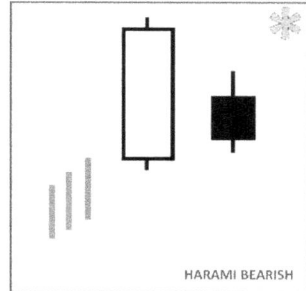

HARAMI BEARISH

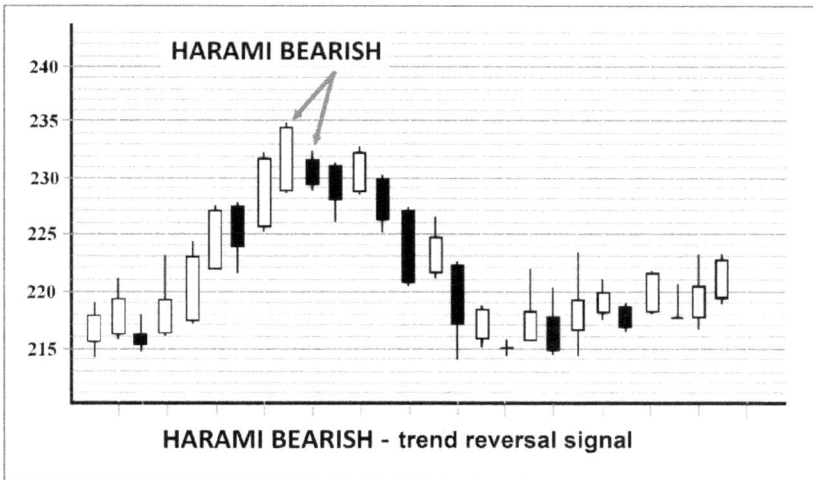

HARAMI BEARISH - trend reversal signal

The sign for reversal trend is even stronger when

1. the small black candle body including shadow, is smaller as the previous white candle;

2. the little black candle body is in the lower zone of the white candle;

3. the white candle totally encloses the black candle, including the possible upper shadow and eventually the lower shadow.

THREE INSIDE DOWN

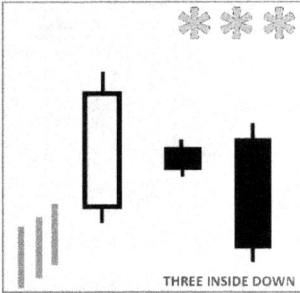

THREE INSIDE DOWN

As the name implies, the THREE INSIDE DOWN consists of three candles which denotes the end of an upward trend.

Composition:
1) The first candle of this configuration is a large white candle.

2) The second trading session ends with a small black candle, which completely fits into the body of the previous white candle. These two candles form a HARAMI BEARISH.

3) In order to reinforce this HARAMI BEARISH and its preview for reversal trend, there is another large black candle formed with a closing price, that is below the closing price of the previous black candle.

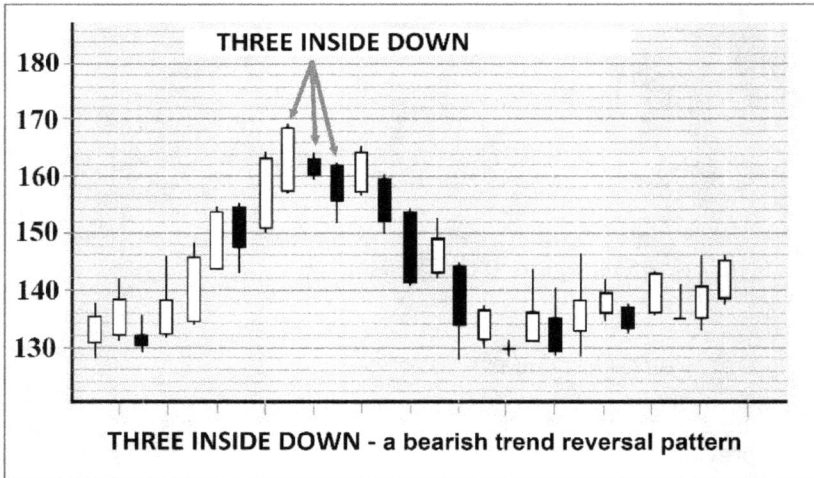

THREE INSIDE DOWN - a bearish trend reversal pattern

The configuration of the THREE SIDE DOWN is a strong signal of an impending trend reversal.

THREE OUTSIDE DOWN

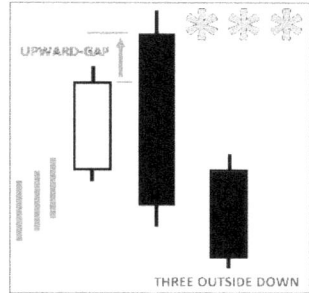

The THREE OUTSIDE DOWN consists of three candles which denotes the end of an upward trend.

This candle configuration is a confirmation of the ENGULFING BEARISH and is for this reason it is sometimes called CONFIRMED BEARISH ENGULFING PATTERN.

Composition:

1) The first candle of this configuration is a large white candle.

2) The second trading session produced a large black candle, which covers the previous white candle fully including the shadows. These two candles forms into an ENGULFING BEARISH.

3) The third trading session produced another black candle which begins with an opening price that was also the same opening price of the white candle.

The THREE OUTSIDE DOWN is a very strong signal and declares the end of the upward trend.

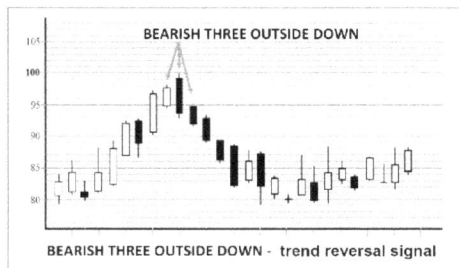

BEARISH THREE OUTSIDE DOWN - trend reversal signal

THREE BLACK CROWS

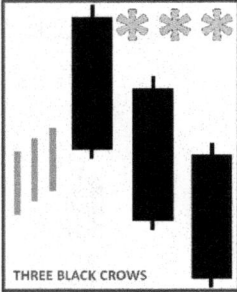

The THREE BLACK CROWS is a strong candle signal of change in trend.

Market logic: The stock brokers realizes that the recent rates were considerably higher than the real value. They induce a greater correction of the course.

THREE BLACK CROWS

Composition:

1) The market is in an upward trend.
2) Are formed by three large consecutive black candles.
3) Each new black candle opens inside the previous black candle body.
4) Any trading session ends with a closing price, which is always lower than the closing price of the previous setting.

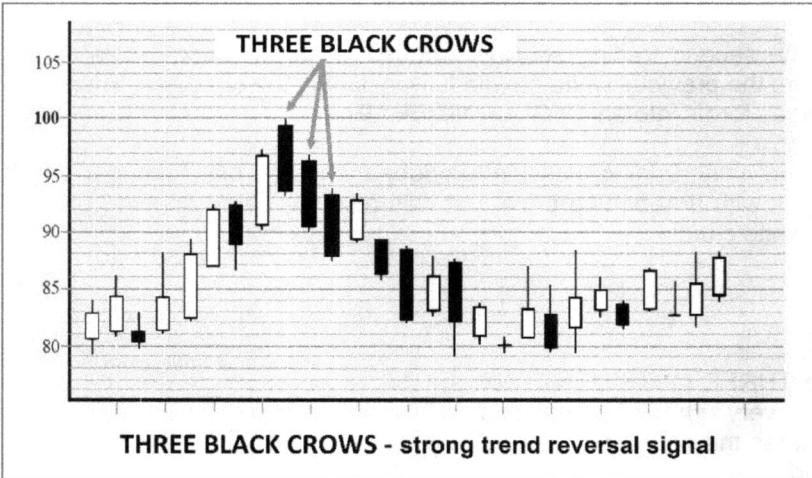

THREE BLACK CROWS - strong trend reversal signal

The THREE BLACK CROWS is a very strong trend change signal.

EVENING STAR

The constellation of EVENING STAR ended mostly in the preceding uptrend.

Market logic: The share price has reached a level at which the buyers become doubtful. After a period of uncertainty, expressed by the excessive placed STAR, the stock brokers try to find a real price in a downward movement.

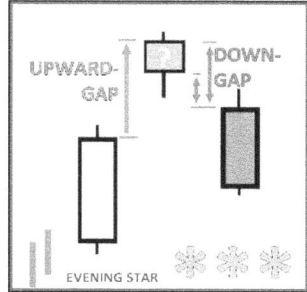

Composition:

1. The first trading session of this candle combination ends even with a big white candle.
2. The following second trading session begins with a significant UP WARD-GAP (windows up). The candle has a small body and has only a small upper shadow and a small lower shadow. The candle can be either black or white.
3. The third trading session begins with a DOWN GAP (down window). During the trading session, the price sinks deep into the white body of the first trading session.

Three properties determine the strength of this signal:

1. The smaller the candle body, (including shadows), in the second trading session, (the STAR), the stronger is the signal;
2. the greater the DOWN GAP is in the third trading session, the stronger is the signal;
3. the more penetration of the black candle body in the third trading session into the white body of the first trading session, the stronger is the signal.

CAUTION: The signal loses its strength when the black candle of the third trading session DOES NOT begin with a DOWN GAP.

This graph shows the EVENING STAR, described on the previous page:

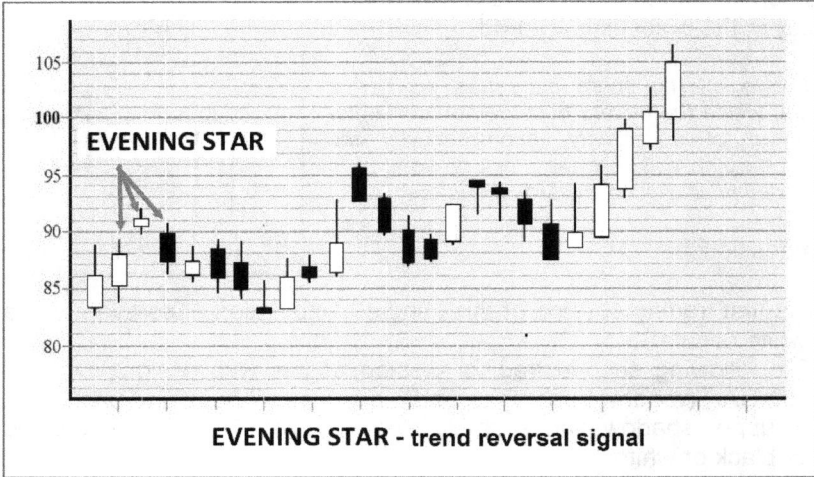

EVENING STAR

EVENING STAR - trend reversal signal

This graph shows the EVENING STAR DOJI, described on the next page:

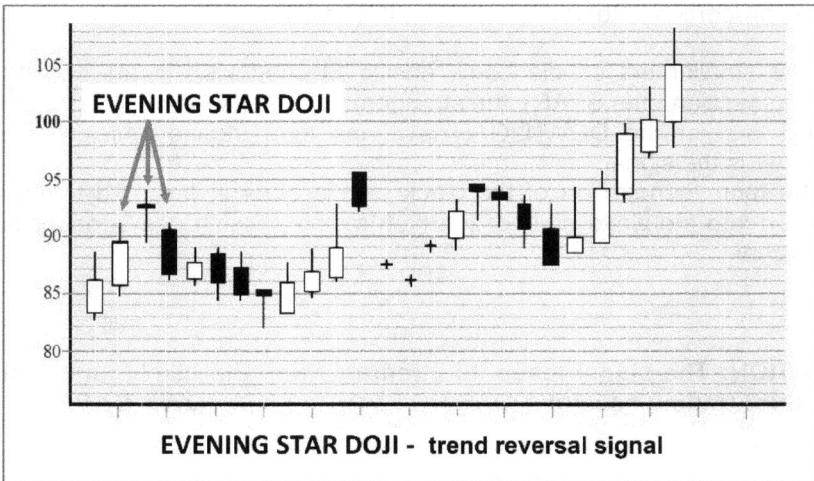

EVENING STAR DOJI

EVENING STAR DOJI - trend reversal signal

EVENING STAR DOJI

The candle combination EVENING STAR DOJI is more expressive than the ordinary EVENING STAR and denotes, in most cases a reversal trend to downwards.

Market logic: The share price has reached a level at which the buyers receive doubts. After a period of uncertainty, expressed by the excessive placed STAR, the stockbrokers tries to find a real price in a downward movement.

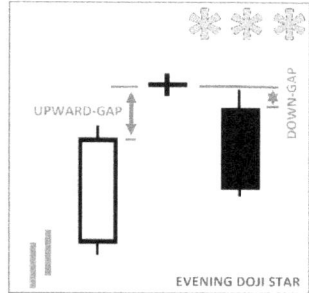

UPWARD-GAP

DOWN-GAP

EVENING DOJI STAR

Composition:

1. The first trading session of this candle combination ends even with a big white candle.

2. The following second trading session begins with a significant UP WARD-GAP (windows up). The candle body is a DOJI with only little shadows.

3. The third trading session begins with a DOWN GAP (down window). During the trading session, the price sinks deep into the white body of the first trading session.

Two characteristics determine the strength of this signal:

1. the greater is the black candle body of the third trading session, the stronger the signal is;

2. the more of the black candle body in the third trading session penetrates into the white body of the first trading session, the stronger is the signal.

CAUTION: The signal loses its strength when the black candle of the third trading session DOES NOT begin with a DOWN GAP.

ABANDONED BABY BEARISH

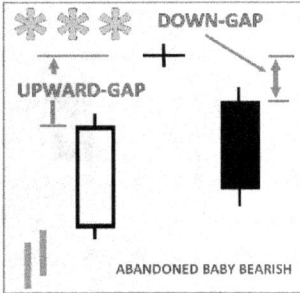

ABANDONED BABY BEARISH

The ABANDONED BABY BEARISH resembles the EVENING STAR DOJI, only in the position of the DOJI but its lower shadow is different.

However, it also signals an end to the upward trend.

Composition:

1. The first trading session of this candle combination ends even with a big white candle.

2. The following second trading session begins with a significant UP WARD-GAP (windows up). The candle body is a DOJI with little upper or lower shadow.

> *A characteristic feature of this candle combination is that neither the upper shadow of the white candle nor the upper shadow of the last black candle, touches below the DOJI located in lower shadow. Hence the name of "orphaned baby" comes.*

ABANDONED BABY BEARISH - signal for trend reversal

3. The third trading session begins with a DOWN GAP (down window). During the trading session, the price falls far into the white body of the first trading session.

UPSIDE TASUKI GAP

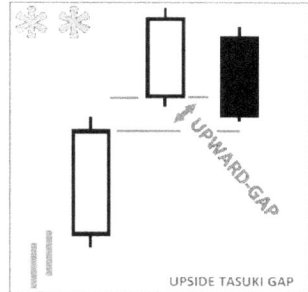

UPSIDE TASUKI GAP

Despite a black candle, this figure combination is considered a sign of continuity, the upward trend continues unhindered.

Composition:

1) The UPSIDE TASUKI GAP begins with a very large white candle.

2) The second trading session begins with an UPWARD-GAP (windows up), and continues the upward trend.

3) The third trading session presents itself as a pseudo-inversion with a black candle. The opening price is somewhat below the closing price of the previous trading session (second white candle).

Important: The window (Upward-GAP) between the two white candles is not an indicative of the black candle or its lower shadow.

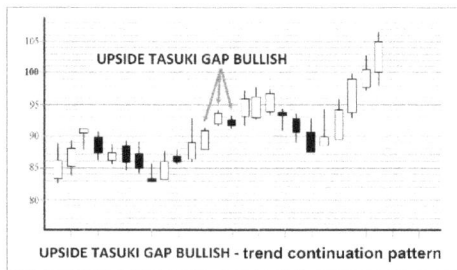

UPSIDE TASUKI GAP BULLISH - trend continuation pattern

The UPSIDE TASUKI GAP absolutely requires a confirmation of the continuation of the upward trend in a next trading session.

The opening of this following trading session must take place over the closing price of the black candle. The DOWN-GAP between the second white candle and the third black candle must not be closed.

UPSIDE GAP THREE METHODS

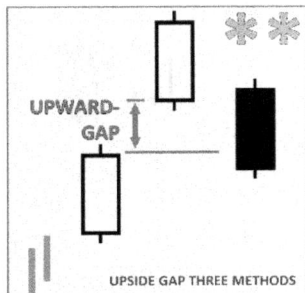

UPSIDE GAP THREE METHODS

Despite the presence of a black candle, this figure combination is considered as a sign of continuity, the upward trend continues unhindered.

Composition:

1) The UPSIDE GAP THREE METHODS begins with a very large white candle.

2) The second trading session begins with an UPWARD-GAP (windows up), and continues the upward trend.

3) The third trading session is a consolidation of the market. The black candle starts inside the body of the previous white candle. One can view this as a pseudo-inverse signal. The black candle body closes the between the two white candles existing GAP. It must not excessively enter in the inside of the first white candle body.

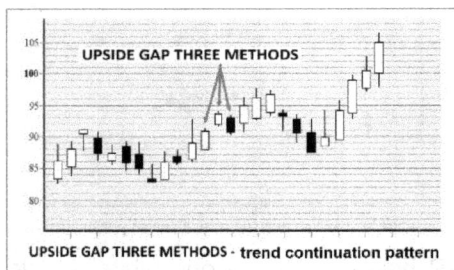

UPSIDE GAP THREE METHODS · trend continuation pattern

The UPSIDE GAP THREE METHODS absolutely requires a confirmation of the continuation of the upward trend at the following trading sessions.

Many market players sees this candle combination as a signal of reversal trend.

THREE LINE STRIKE BULLISH

The candle combination THREE LINE STRIKE BULLISH is considered despite the presence of a black candle as a sign of continuation for the upward trend.

BULLISH THREE LINES STRIKE

Composition:

1) The THREE LINE STRIKE BULLISH begins with three consecutive large white candles.

2) After these three white candles follows an excessively large black candle that completely covers all previous three white candles' bodies. The closing price of the black candle is not higher than the opening of the first of the three white candles.

Market logic: Despite massive counter force, the price increase cannot be stopped. Demand is too important.

The candle combination THREE LINE STRIKE BULLISH is regarded as a signal of continuity for price trend.

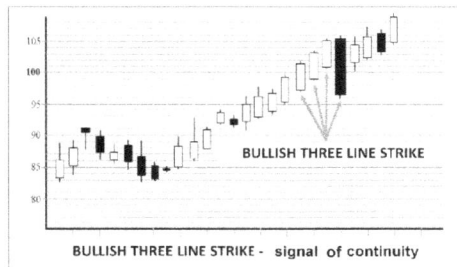

BULLISH THREE LINE STRIKE

BULLISH THREE LINE STRIKE - signal of continuity

The reliability of this signal is, however, regarded as mediocre. Confirmation must bring the following trading sessions.

THIRD CHAPTER - #3

TREND: upward
LAST CANDLE: white

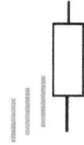

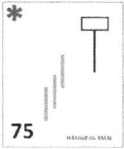

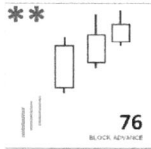

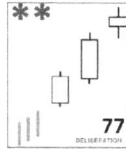

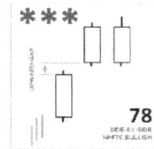

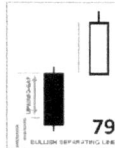

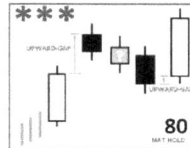

75 HANGING MAN

76 BLOCK ADVANCE

77 DELIBERATION

78 SIDE-BY-SIDE WHITE BULLISH

79 BULLISH SEPARATING LINE

80 MAT HOLD

WHITE HANGING MAN

White or black, the HANGING MAN appears always in two colors in an upward trend.

Without upper shadow but with a very long lower shadow and a short body, the HANGING MAN is identical to the figure of HAMMERS. Difference: HAMMERS appears only in downtrends.

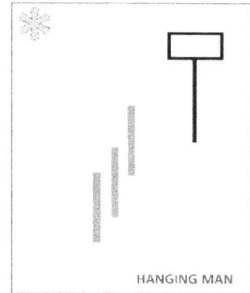

HANGING MAN

Important: The lower shadow should be at least twice as large as the candle body.

Market logic: Probably due to a market rumor, the course rushes shortly after trading session opening in the depth. The rumor did not hold a further investigation. The course can be improved again during the trading session, so that the closing price is very close to opening price.

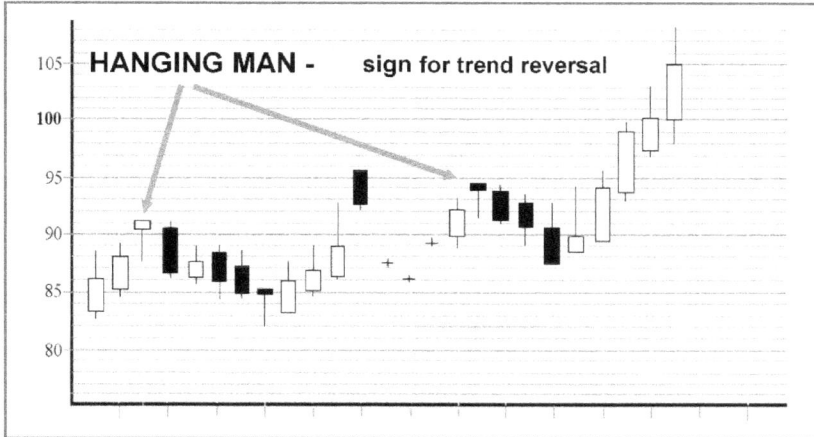

The HANGING MAN can be a very strong signal of trend reversal. However, this must be confirmed in the next trading session by a black candle.

ADVANCE BLOCK

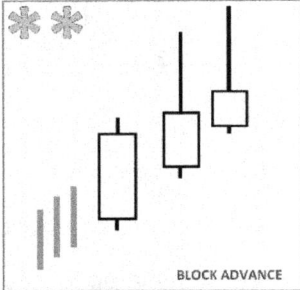

BLOCK ADVANCE

The ADVANCE BLOCK consists of three white candles, but it denotes the end of the upward trend and is therefore a signal for reversal trend.

Configuration:

1) The opening prices of all three white candles are invariably inside the previous candle body.

2) The size of the candles decreases constantly. The following candle is always slightly less than the previous.

3) The upper shadows above the second and third white candles are relatively long. These long upper shadows must be interpreted as a signal for reversal trend.

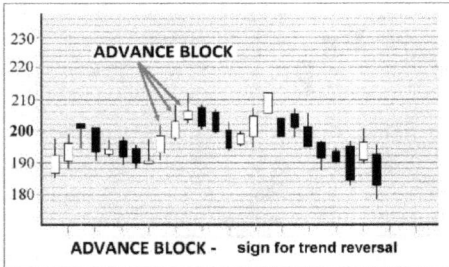

ADVANCE BLOCK - sign for trend reversal

The ADVANCE BLOCK stops the upward trend. However, this must be confirmed by a black candle in the following trading session.

DELIBERATION

The candle configuration DELIBERATION consists of three white candles and expresses the indecision of the market operators after several trading sessions in uptrend.

It resembles the BEARISH ADVANCE BLOCK, but differs in shape and position, particularly the third white candle.

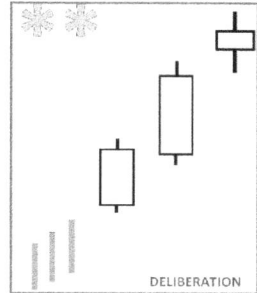

DELIBERATION

Configuration:

1) The first white candle is not particularly large.

2) The second white candle surpasses the size of the first candle, even considerably larger than they appear.

3) The third white candle is small and like a star, it's positioned significantly higher or only slightly projecting into the second candle.

Both the shadows, whether long or short, are not meaningful at all.

Important:
If the last third white candle is a **DOJI;** it will change the signal of uncertainty to a signal of consolidation.

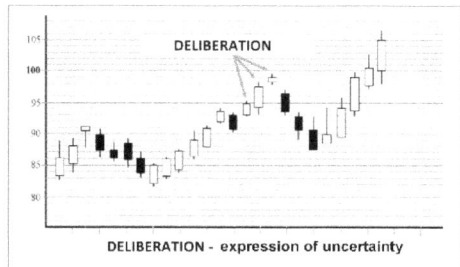

DELIBERATION - expression of uncertainty

77

SIDE-BY-SIDE WHITE LINE BULLISH

The candle combination SIDE-BY-SIDE WHITE LINE BULLISH is a strong signal of continuity to pursue the upward trend.

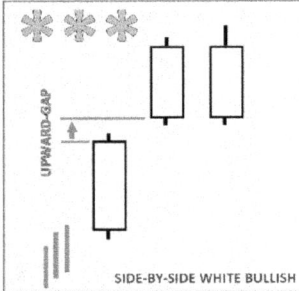

Composition:

1) In an uptrend, a large white candle is followed by another white candle. This second white candle is positioned above an UPWARD-GAP to the first white candle.

2) This second white candle is copied during the third trading session. Important: the upper shadow of the third white candle is greater than the upper shadow of the second candle.

Market logic: The first big white candle expresses the will of the market operators to pursue the upward trend. The second trading session begins with an UPWARD-GAP (windows up), and testifies that buyers are willing to accept higher prices. The third trading session endorses the behavior of market players in the previous meetings and witnessed willingness to accept further price increases as seen in the higher upper shadow.

In particular, the third candle reinforces the strong signal to continue the upward trend.

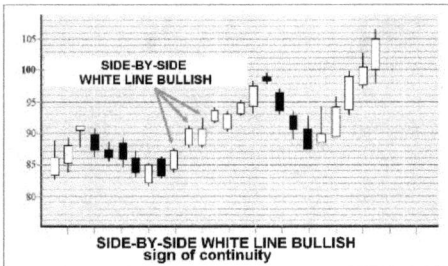

SIDE-BY-SIDE WHITE LINE BULLISH
sign of continuity

Nevertheless, a confirmation in the session following with another that the fourth white candle is desirable before taking up a position.

BULLISH SEPARATING LINE

The figure BULLISH SEPARATING LINE is, despite the presence of a black candle, a constellation of continuity.

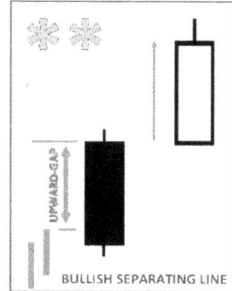

BULLISH SEPARATING LINE

Composition:

1) After several sessions in an upward trend, a new session begins with a large UPWARD-GAP, in which the course strongly falls again to the vicinity of the body of the previous candle. The closing price of the black candle is located approximately at the level of the closing price of the previous candle.

2) The second trading session, (in the drawing the white candle), has the same opening price as the previous trading session, (...see black candle). During this trading session, the price rises sharply.

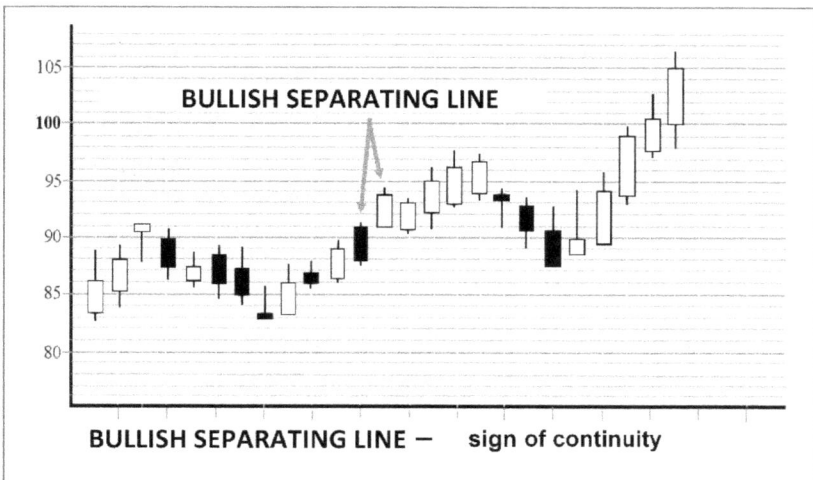

BULLISH SEPARATING LINE — sign of continuity

Despite the presence of a black candle, there is a constellation of continuity.

MAT HOLD or RISING THREE METHODS

The candle combination MAT HOLD or RISING THREE METHODS consists of five candles of distinct colors. It is a signal of continuity.

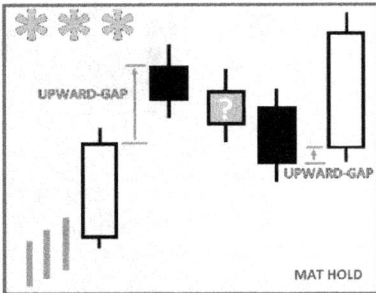

Configuration:
1) The first candle is white and very large.

2) 3) 4) Starting with an UPWARD-GAP to present three smaller mostly black candles, (the third candle of MAT HOLD may also be white).

5) The fifth candle is white and very large. This fifth trading session opened with an UPWARD-GAP and thus has an opening rate slightly higher than the closing price of the previous setting.

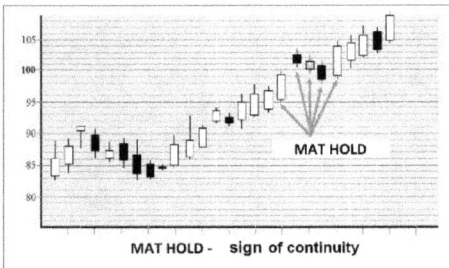

MAT HOLD - sign of continuity

The constellation MAT HOLD or RISING THREE METHODS is a strong signal that expresses the progress of the upward trend.

CHAPTER FOUR - #4

TREND: downward
LAST CANDLE: black

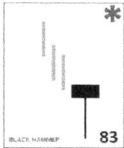

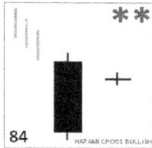

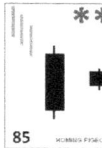

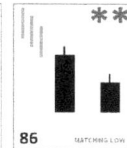

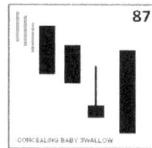

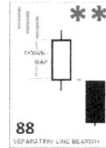

BLACK HAMMER   83

HARAMI CROSS BULLISH   84

HOMING PIGEON   85

MATCHING LOW   86

CONCEALING BABY SWALLOW   87

DOWN GAP   88   SEPARATING LINE BEARISH

BLACK HAMMER

The figures BLACK HAMMER and HANGING MAN are identical. They are also probably the most known figures of the candlestick charts.

At the end of a downtrend this figure is called BLACK HAMMER; at the end of an uptrend, it is called HANGING MAN.

Both figures can be black or white.

The HAMMER consists of a small body with a very long lower shadow. The lower shadow must be at least twice as large as the candle body.

BLACK HAMMER

The HAMMER can be a very strong signal for a trend change; especially if the following candle has a white body.

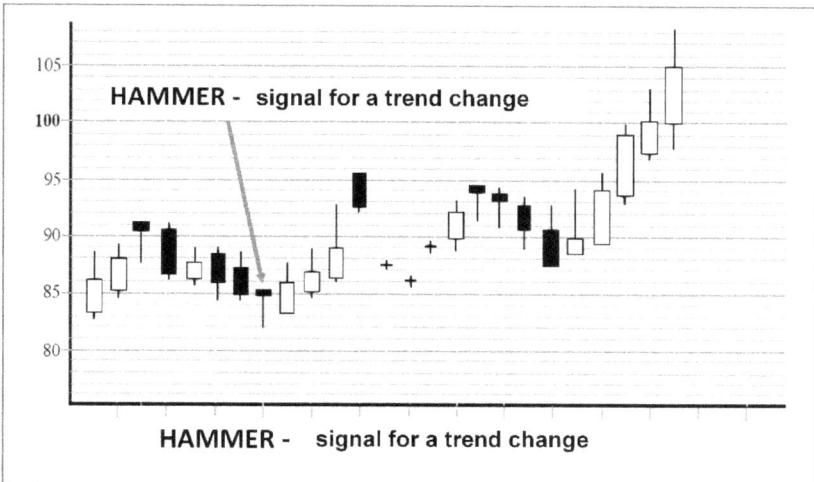

HAMMER - signal for a trend change

HAMMER - signal for a trend change

Warning: Some traders, however, see the HAMMER as a WRONG SIGNAL and advise to take caution!

HARAMI CROSS BULLISH

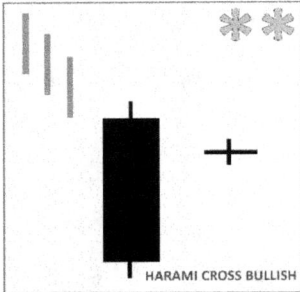

After a long downtrend the HARAMI CROSS BULLISH signaled an impending reversal trend.

Market logic: After several trading sessions in downtrend, it sets a balance between supply and demand.
If at the next meeting the DOJI is followed by a white candle, the former sellers change its position and they buy their sold shares back.
Due to the increased buying demand, the price rises in the following trading sessions.

The reverse signal is stronger so as to,

1. insofar as the DOJI is in the upper zone of the black candle;

2. if the black candle body covers the DOJI including its shadow.

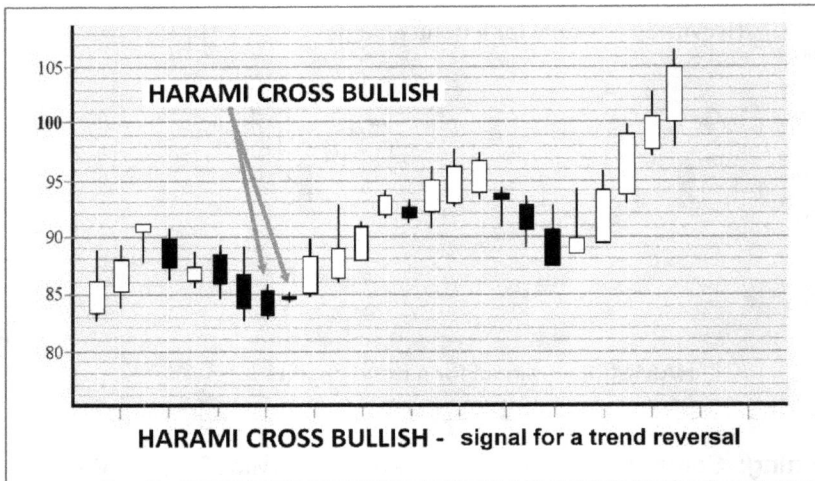

HARAMI CROSS BULLISH - signal for a trend reversal

84

HOMING PIGEON

Normally, two black candles in a downward trend usually identifies further exchange trading sessions in downtrend. But this doesn't need to be the case with the figure, the HOME PIGEON.

Here, a large black candle is followed by a small black candle which is placed inside the body of the first black candle.

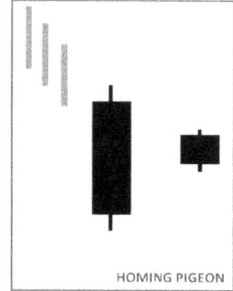

HOMING PIGEON

If it shows up at the next trading session a significant size white candle, (which happens very often), so the HOMING PIGEON announces a change in trend.

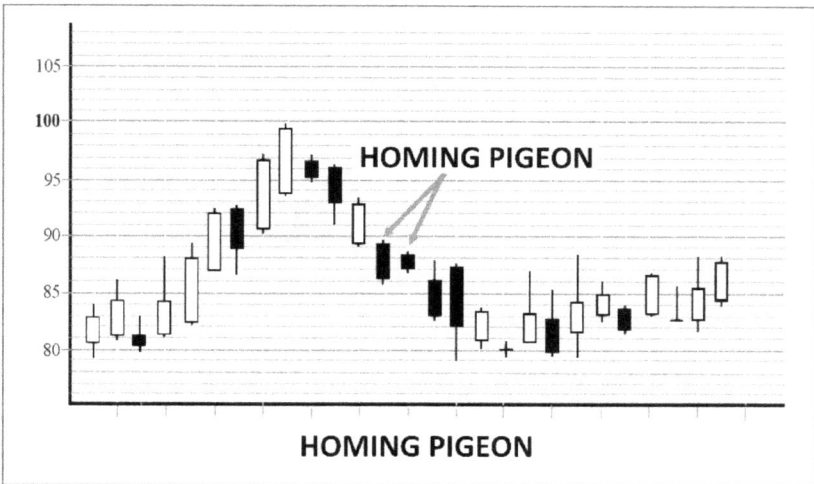

HOMING PIGEON

HOMING PIGEON

As can be seen from the graph, the HOMING PIGEON is followed by a black candle. This candle combination may, but doesn't need to show a reverse tendency!

MATCHING LOW

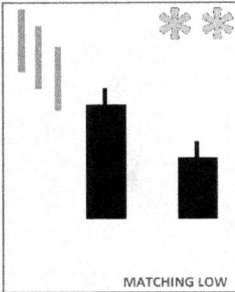

MATCHING LOW

The MATCHING LOW candle combination is consists of two black candles and is a sign of an impending reversal trend.

The special feature of the MATCHING LOW: Both candles have the same closing price, which is also the lowest price in two trading sessions.

If the MATCHING LOW is regarded as a reversal trend sign towards an upward trend, this low price must be respected in any case.

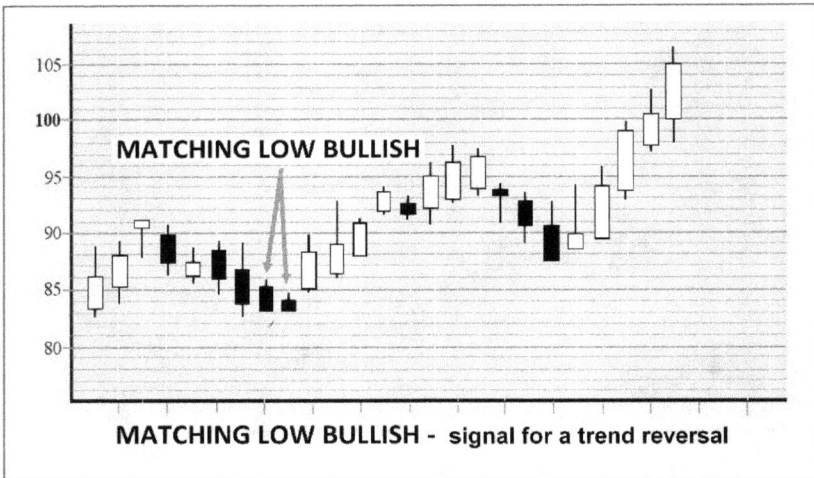

MATCHING LOW BULLISH - signal for a trend reversal

Before taking up a position, however, confirmation should be made through white candles in one or two succeeding trading sessions.

CONCEALING BABY SWALLOW

This candle combination is often seen as a sign of an impending trend change.

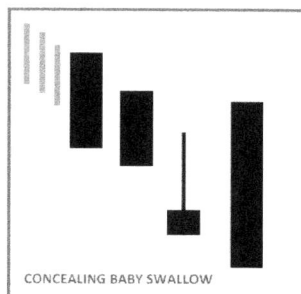

CONCEALING BABY SWALLOW

But looking at statistics, it is found that this Candles' image is usually a WRONG SIGNAL; so there is no sign of an impending reversal trend.

Therefore, because of his awareness that CONCEALING BABY SWALLOW is only mentioned here, without allocating it any rating or assessment.

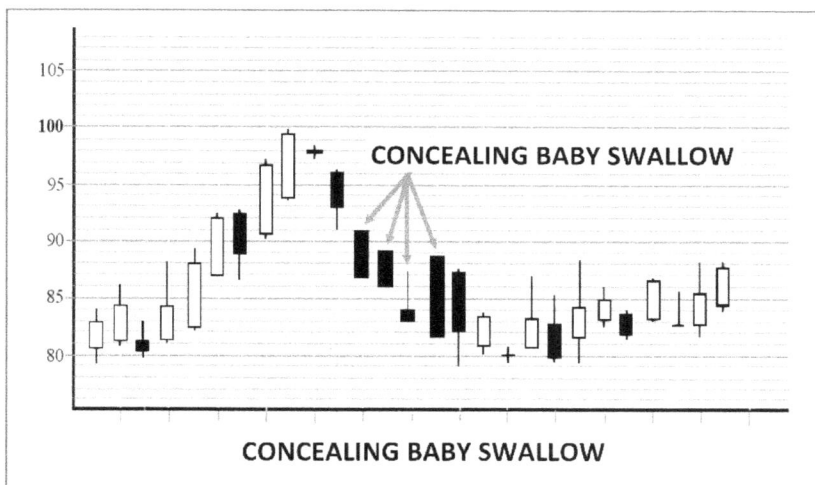

CONCEALING BABY SWALLOW

BEARISH SEPARATING LINE

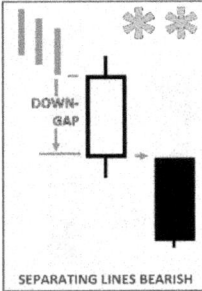

SEPARATING LINES BEARISH

Despite the presence of a white candle, the BEARISH SEPARATING LINE confirms the downtrend.

Composition:

1) The first trading session starts with a large DOWN GAP. The closing price is, however, the same in the amount of the previous candle.

Market logic: The opening price is so low that the amount of the purchase requests proliferated, thus driving the price during the trading session back in height.

2) The second trading session, (black candle), opens with the same opening price as that of the previous trading session, (white candle).

Market logic: The stockbrokers evaluate the rates of previous trading session as too high and start the new trading session on the opening level of the previous trading session. During this trading session, (black candle), it halts the morose mood.

Important: The black candle in no case may have an upper shadow and doesn't matter how small is the lower shadow.

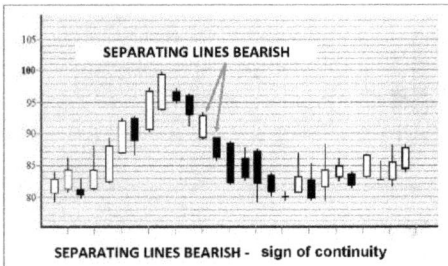

SEPARATING LINES BEARISH - sign of continuity

In this picture the BEARISH SEPARATING LINE is confirmed as a sign of continuity of downward trend.

TREND: downward
LAST CANDLE: white

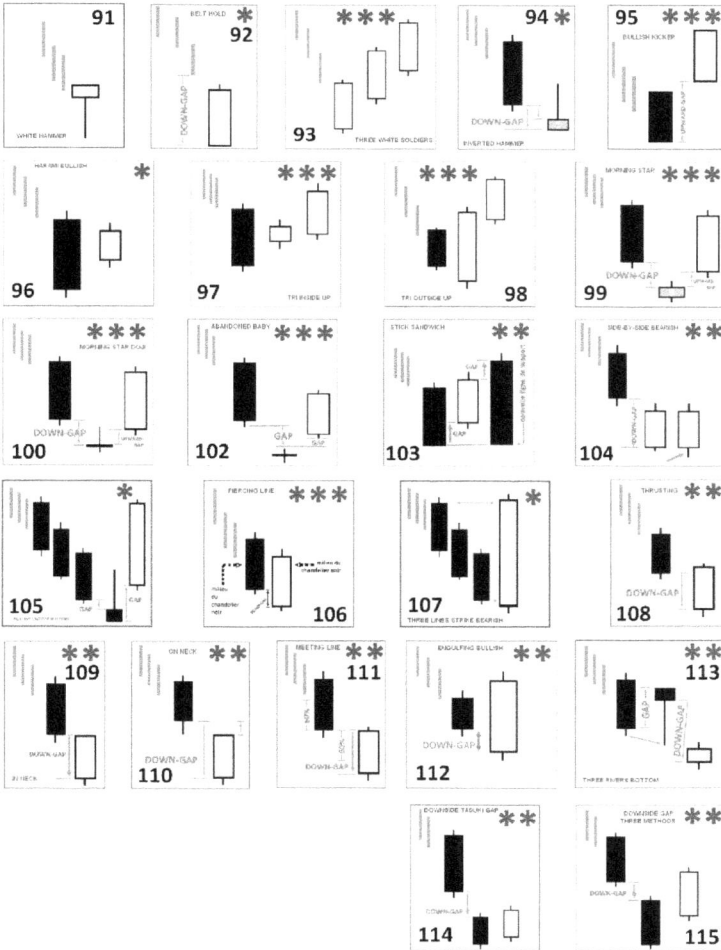

WHITE HAMMER

The figures WHITE HAMMER and HANGING MAN are identical. They are also probably the most known figures of the candlestick charts.

At the end of a downward trend the figure is called WHITE HAMMER; on the other hand if at the end of an upward trend, the figure is called HANGING MAN.

Both figures can be either white and black.

The HAMMER consists of a small body with a very long lower shadow. The lower shadow located beneath the body must be at least twice as large as the candle body.

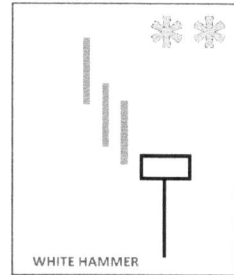

WHITE HAMMER

The HAMMER can be a very strong sign of a trend change; especially if the following candle also has a white body.

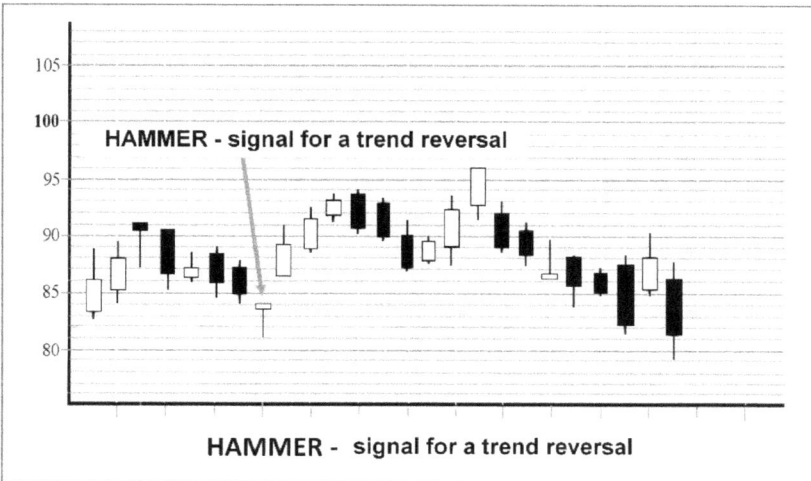

HAMMER - signal for a trend reversal

BELT HOLD BULLISH

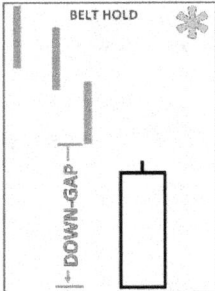

This candle constellation is a sign of a reversal trend and appears rarely in the candle graphics. A WHITE OPENING MARUBOZU appears at the end of a longer series of a course of losing trading sessions.

With a significant DOWN GAP (windows down), a WHITE OPENING MARUBOZU is established, (a white candle, an expression of rising prices). The closing price stabilizes very near to the trading sessions' highest price.

Important: The WHITE OPENING MARUBOZU must not have any lower shadow that is below the opening price. To position itself as a buyer, confirmation should definitely be awaited by the next trading session.

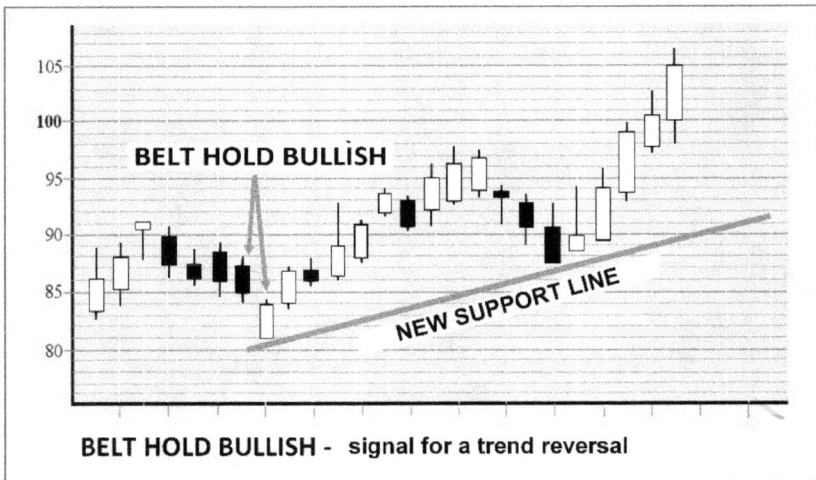

BELT HOLD BULLISH - signal for a trend reversal

The opening price of the BELT HOLD BULLISH often constitutes the very the beginning of an emerging support line for the following trading sessions.

THREE WHITE SOLDIERS

The combination THREE WHITE SOLDIERS is a very strong reversal trend sign.

Composition:

1) In a prolonged downward trend, appears the first large white candle.

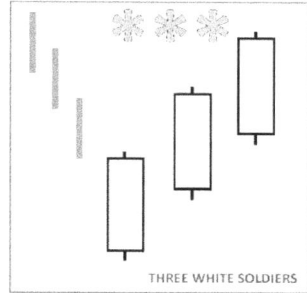

THREE WHITE SOLDIERS

2) The closing prices of the second and third white candles are without exception inside the white candle bodies of the previous trading sessions.

3) The upper shadows above the white candles should be as short as possible.

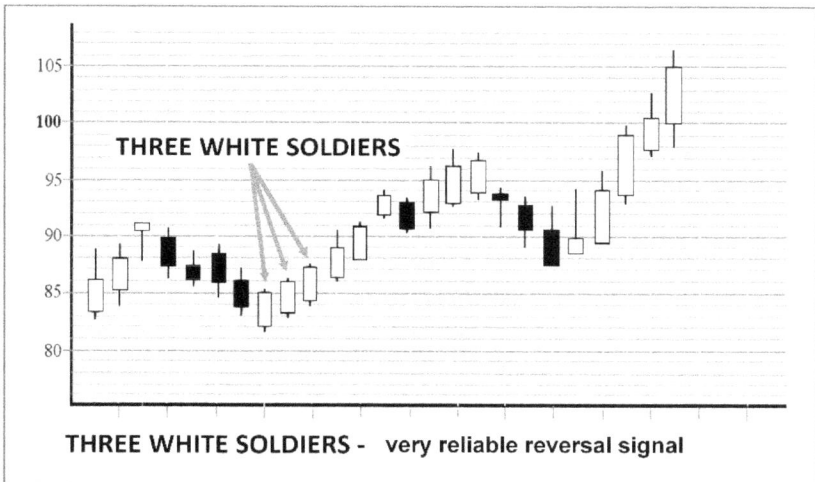

THREE WHITE SOLDIERS -   very reliable reversal signal

This combination THREE WHITE SOLDIERS is a very strong reversal sign to a prolonged uptrend.

INVERTED HAMMER

The INVERTED HAMMER often appears on a downward trend as doubtful evidence of a reversal trend.

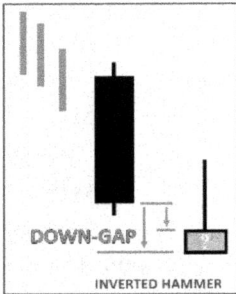

It consists of a single white or black candle with a very little candle body, but above the body it has an oversized upper shadow.

The opening price of an INVERTED HAMMER, (see the DOWN GAP) is significantly lower than the closing price of the previous setting, (black candle).

Market logic: Following the downtrend opens the stockbrokers, the session of the INVERTED HAMMER is far below the previous closing price. However, too large purchase request pushes the price well into the black candle body of the previous trading session.

However, this upward price thrust cannot be stabilized and falls to the end of trading session to a level close to the opening price, with a white candle above the opening price and a black candle slightly below the opening price.

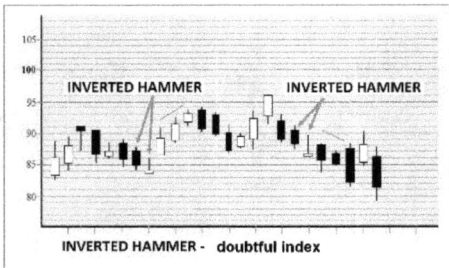

The INVERTED HAMMER requires attention, but is only a very feeble sign of inversion and must receive confirmation in the following trading sessions before the market players can take an opinion.

BULLISH KICKER

This candle combination is a relatively safe reversal trend sign.

In this candle combination, the previous trend plays only a small role.

> *Market logic: The BULLISH KICKER appears in graphic at the most surprising information about the related market value.*

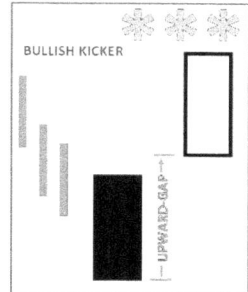

Composition:

1) In a prolonged downward trend, a very large black candle is positioned.

2) In a distinct UPWARD-GAP (…see market logic) begins an equally large white candle without shadows, a WHITE MARUBOZU. This trading session ends with the trading session's highest price.

One must note that the candle combination BULLISH KICKER, (so two candles without shadows), is founded only very rarely in the graphics.

The BULLISH KICKER is a very strong and relatively reliable signal of a positive change in trend.

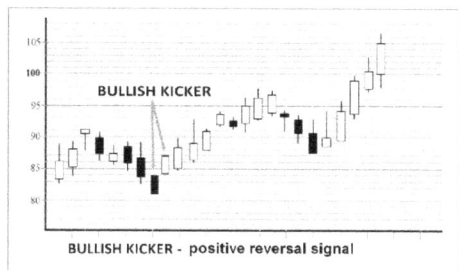

BULLISH KICKER - positive reversal signal

HARAMI BULLISH

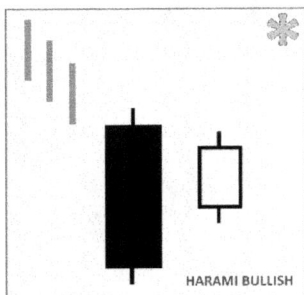

HARAMI BULLISH

Placed at the end of a series of trading session in a downward trend, the BULLISH HARAMI is a sign of trend reversal.

Market logic: Every occurrence to stop the long-term price decline is the market players welcome. This can be a finding of undervaluation of the quoted paper, or even an unexpected market rumor. The candle combination HARAMI BULLISH illustrates the tendency of the market operators, a turnaround to accept willingly.

Composition:

1) In a long-term downward trend, a large black candle is shown.

2) The second white candle is so small that it fully fits into the body of the previous black candle (including its own shadows).

The BULLISH HARAMI is a sign of reversal trend with a moderate reliability. Therefore a confirmation is always necessary.

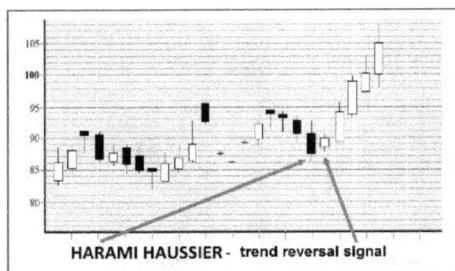

HARAMI HAUSSIER - trend reversal signal

The signl is emphasized in reliability when the small white candle fits in the upper part of the previous black candle.

96

THREE INSIDE UP

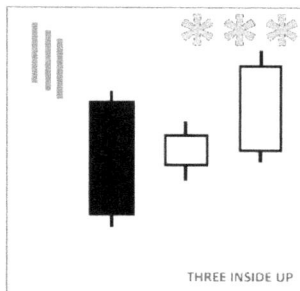

THREE INSIDE UP

This candle combination always ends in a continuing downward trend over several trading sessions.

Composition:

1) The first trading session ends with a big black candle.

2) The second trading session is formed with a small white candle, a HARAMI BULLISH.

3) The third trading session begins with an opening price that is inside the previous small white candle. During this trading session, the price rises strongly and closes above the black candle including its upper shadow.

> *Market logic: After a period of indecision, market operators have their win of confidence in the second trading session and regain increase in their purchase requests. The greater the demand, the higher the price.*

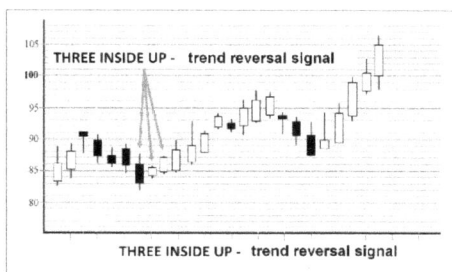

THREE INSIDE UP - trend reversal signal

If the figure HARAMI BULLISH is already a sign for reversal trend, so the candle combination THREE INSIDE UP brings the confirmation.

Therefore, this figure is also called **CONFIRMED** HARAMI BULLISH.

THREE OUTSIDE UP

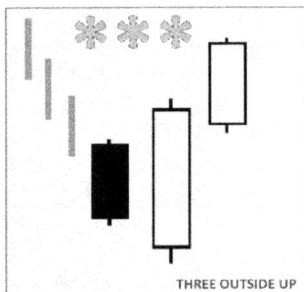

THREE OUTSIDE UP

The candle combination THREE OUTSIDE UP is a strong trend reversal sign.

Configuration:

1) A black candle concludes the series of negative trading sessions.

2) The first white candle has a size that covers at least the entire body including the shadows of the previous black candle.

3) The third trading session opens with a price which is located in the upper part of the previous white candle. The closing price of the second white candle is far above the closing price of its predecessor.

4) The upper shadows of the two white candles should be as small as possible.

The configuration of THREE OUTDOOR BULL, often called THREE OUTSIDE UP, is a very strong sign of reversal trend.

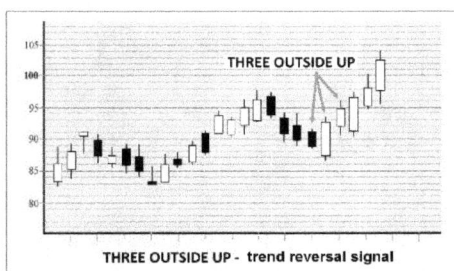

THREE OUTSIDE UP - trend reversal signal

After a sustained series of negative trading sessions, the THREE OUTSIDE UP indicated clearly to turn to bullish direction INCREASE, (upward trend).

MORNING STAR

The MORNING STAR often appears at the end of a prolonged downward movement.

Configuration:

1) A long black candle testifies to an excessively large sales offer and little interest from buyers.

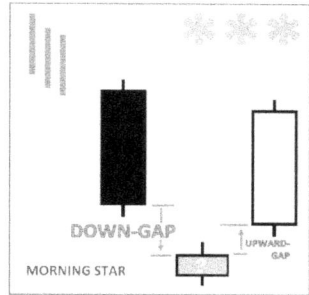

2) The second trading session begins with a clear DOWN GAP (windows down). A small candle body with little upper and lower shadows expresses the uncertainty of the market operators and their displeasure at the course level. The color of these candles may be white, but may also be black. Color plays only a minor role.

3) The third trading session, a long white candle, begins with an UPWARD-GAP. The closing price of this white candle should be as much as possible closer to the opening price of the black candle or this would even surpass it. The MORNING STAR loses its signal effect, if this third trading session does not begin with an UPWARD-GAP.

Three characteristics that defines the strength of MORNING STAR as a sign of reversal trend:

1. The smaller the second candle (including the shadows), the stronger the signal.

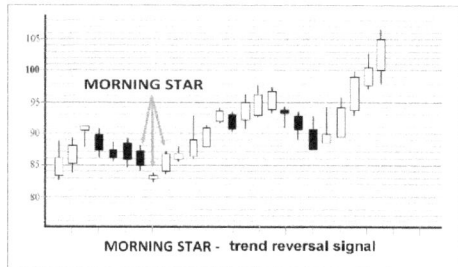

MORNING STAR - trend reversal signal

2. The greater the UPWARD-GAP by the third trading session, the stronger the signal.

3. The more the body of the third candle assumes the size of the first black candle, or even dominate it in size, the stronger the signal.

MORNING STAR DOJI

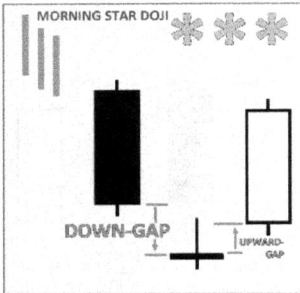

More significant than the MORNING STAR is MORNING STAR DOJI in its function as a sign of a reversal trend.

Configuration:

1) A long black candle testifies to an excessively large sales offer and little interest from buyers.

2) The second trading session begins with a clear DOWN GAP (windows down). The candle body is a DOJI with little lower shadow and a little greater upper shadow. It expresses the uncertainty of market players and their displeasure at the price level.

3) The third trading session, (a long white candle), begins with an UPWARD-GAP. The closing price of this white candle should be as much as possible closer to the opening price of the black candle or this even surpasses it.

The MORNING STAR loses his signal effect, if this third trading session does not begin with an UPWARD-GAP.

Two characteristics that defines the strength of MORNING STAR DOJI as a sign of reversal trend:

1. The greater the UPWARD-GAP in the third trading session, the stronger is the signal.

2. The more the body of the third candle assumes the size of the first black candle, or even dominate in size, the stronger the signal.

This chart shows the MORNING STAR DOJI of the previous page.

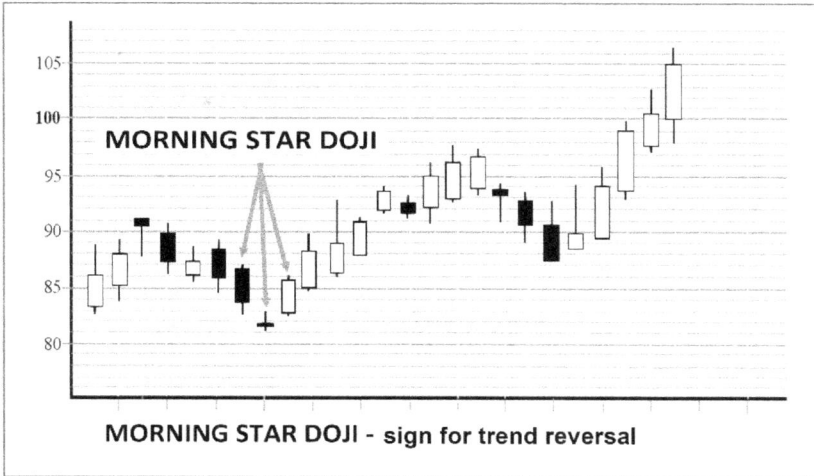

MORNING STAR DOJI

MORNING STAR DOJI - sign for trend reversal

ABANDONED BABY BULLISH

ABANDONED BABY BULLISH - trend reversal signal

This chart shows the ABANDONED BABY BULLISH of the following page.

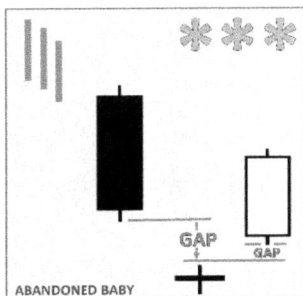

The ABANDONED BABY BULLISH is a trend reversal sign.

Composition:

1) In a downtrend is formed a large black candle.

2) The ensuing trading session begins with a DOWN GAP (windows down). The candle body is a DOJI with only short upper and lower shadows.

3) The third trading session begins with an UPWARD-GAP (windows up). During this trading session, the rate greatly increases to a maximum to fill the body of the black candle.

In this configuration, a special regard is considered given the shadows:

1. Between the lower shadow of the black candle, the lower shadow of white candle and the upper shadow of the DOJI exist a GAP, (window). It may therefore be no contact between the three figures, black candle, white candle and DOJI.

For this reason this configuration is called ABANDONED BABY.

The configuration of ABANDONED BABY BULLISH is considered a strong reversal trend sign.

STICK SANDWICH

The STICK SANDWICH is regarded as a sign of an impending trend reversal.

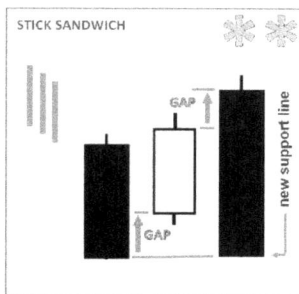

Composition:

1) In a downward trend is formed a large black candle without lower shadow!

2) The ensuing trading session begins with an UPWARD-GAP (windows up). The opening price is higher than the closing price of the previous setting. This session creates a large white candle.

3) The third trading session begins again with an UPWARD-GAP, but the price will suffer a huge drop. This third trading session concludes with the lowest price, which corresponds to the closing price of the first trading session (first black candle).

Market logic: Since the two black candles do not have lower shadows, stock brokers assumes that starting by the two closing prices of the black candles, a newly defined support line will be created. If the price decreases no lower than the following trading sessions, so only then it can be presumed an upward movement in prices or a neutral trend.

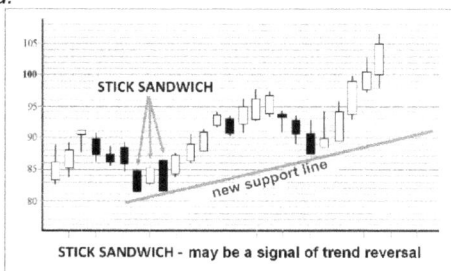

The reliability of the prediction of STICK SANDWICH is mediocre. Therefore, a confirmation is necessary.

STICK SANDWICH - may be a signal of trend reversal

Important: If any of the two black candles have a lower shadow, that is it ever so small, then a continuation of the downward trend is feared.

SIDE-BY-SIDE WHITE LINE BEARISH

This candle combination in a downward trend represents continuity of this downtrend.

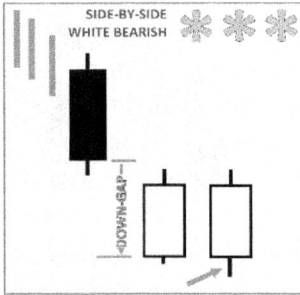

Composition:

1) The starting position is a big black candlestick following a prolonged downtrend.

2) The second trading session begins with a DOWN GAP (windows down), and creates a white candle.

3) At the third trading session, it produces an exact copy of the previous white candle with a significant difference: the lower shadow is longer than the lower shadow of the white candle of the second trading session.

Market logic: The first candle, (the black candle), testifies to the downward trend. In the second trading session, a price crash takes place at the beginning as represented by the DOWN-GAP, but immediately corrected by a sharp increase in the purchase demand. However, the rate cannot reach the closing price of the previous trading session and leaves a window between the black and the first white candle. This expresses the readiness of the market operators from accepting a price decline and hence the downtrend.

The third trading session is a confirmation of the previous trading session history, and the longer lower shadow emphasizes the willingness of the market actors to accept the continuation of the downward trend.

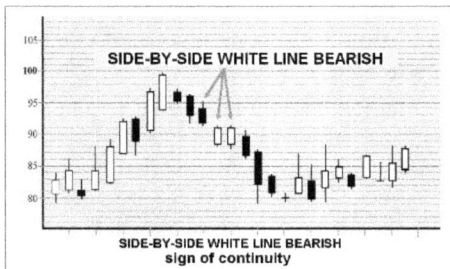

Next to this SIDE-BY-SIDE WHITELINE BEARISH is another black candle, so this should be seen as confirmation.

BULLISH LADDER BOTTOM

This candle combination indicates a trend change to bullish.

Composition:

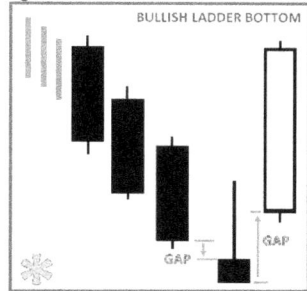

1) In a longer-lasting downtrend are three black most imposing candles.

2) After the third big black candle starts a trading session with a DOWN GAP (windows down). The trading session concludes with an INVERTED HAMMER.

3) The fifth to be considered trading session, (the first and only white candle), begins with a clear UPWARD-GAP (windows up). The size of the white candle is impressive because of the closing price of this white candle is identical to the opening price of the first black candle.

Market logic: Over a long period of time, the market players have accepted falling prices. A basic rule of the financial market, however, includes that after each downward trend follows an upward trend as long as no extraordinary event must be listed. The INVERTED HAMMER is the expected alarm.

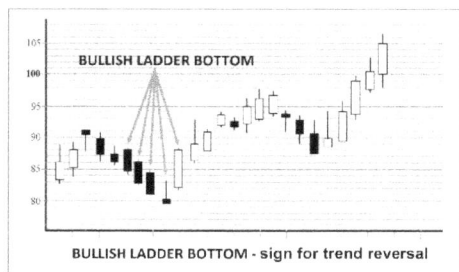

The large white candle and its UPWARD-GAP brings the confirmation of the trend change. However, it should appear as a white candle in the succeeding trading session.

BULLISH LADDER BOTTOM - sign for trend reversal

105

PIERCING LINE

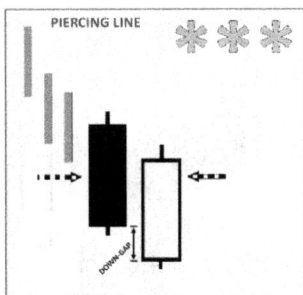

The PIERCING LINE is a sign of reversal trend.

Composition:

1) A long black candle in the downward trend is the starting position.

2) The following trading session opens with a very respectable DOWN GAP (windows down). During this second trading session, the price rises to more than half of the previous black candle body. The closing price of the white candle is also above the half black candle body.

As it corresponds the graph of the composition; this is a relatively strong sign for reversal trend.

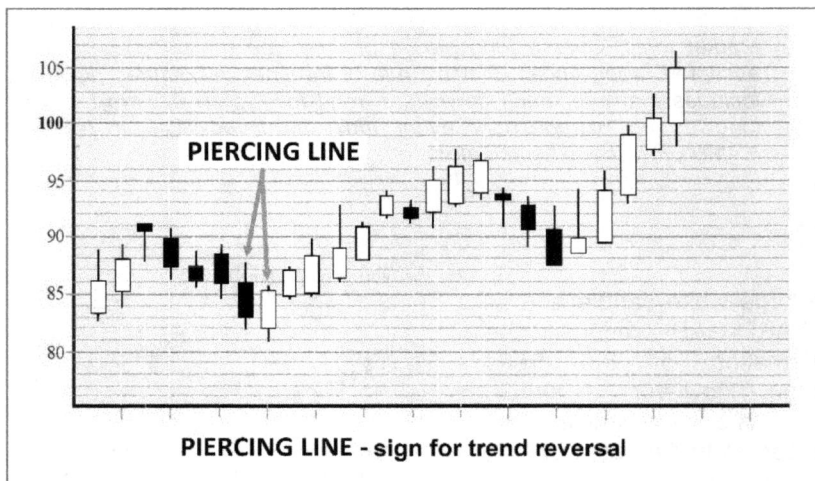

PIERCING LINE - sign for trend reversal

Important: If the closing price of the white candle can not be above the middle of the black candle body, then the PIERCING LINE is a THRUSTING BEARISH and thus a sign for the continuation of the downward trend!

THREE LINES STRIKE BEARISH

This candle composition is a sign of trend continuity.

Composition:

1) In a prolonged downward trend, there are three relatively large black candles whose opening prices are inside the respective previous candles body.

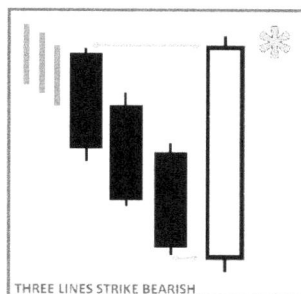

THREE LINES STRIKE BEARISH

2) The fourth candle is an overly large white candle. Its body covers the previous three black candle bodies including their shadows.

> *Market logic: After several negative trading sessions, the stock brokers are trying to halt the downward trend. However, the intention of the seller to avoid further major losses is stronger and the trend continues downward.*

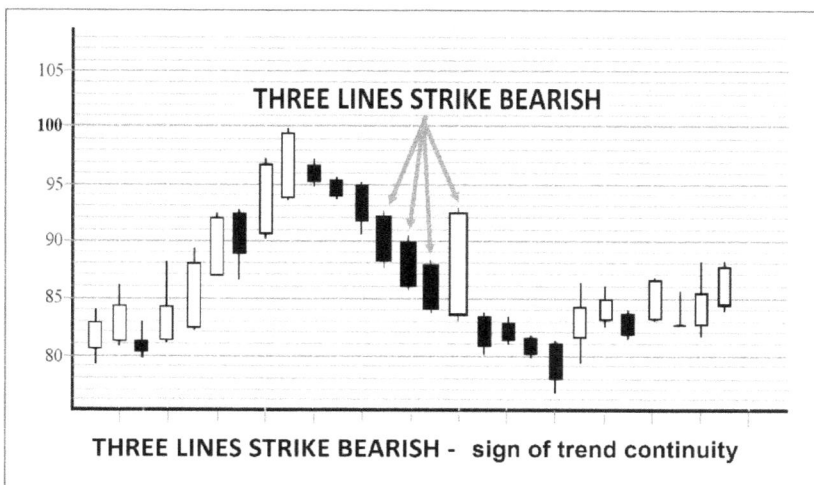

THREE LINES STRIKE BEARISH - sign of trend continuity

THRUSTING BEARISH

The candle combination THRUSTING BEARISH is, despite the presence of a white candle, a sign for the continuation of the downward trend.

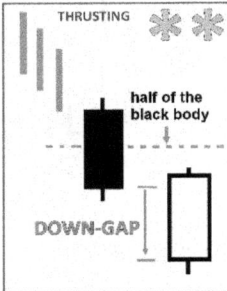

Composition:

1) It must be in a downtrend to be considered a black candle.

2) The second trading session begins with an imposing DOWN GAP. During this trading session, the price rises. The closing price is located inside the body of the previous black candle.

Important: The final price cannot be fixed above the half of the body of the previous black candle.

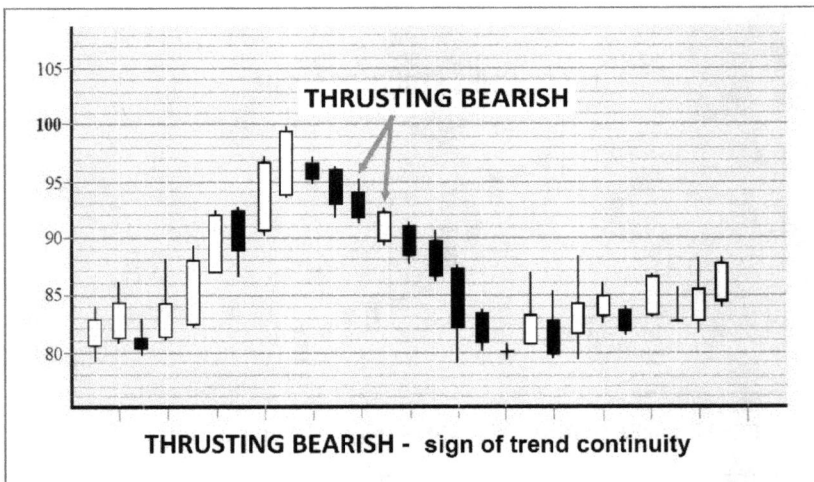

THRUSTING BEARISH - sign of trend continuity

Not to be confused with PIERCING LINE, the combination THRUSTING BEARISH is a sign of continuity.

IN NECK

This candle combination does not interrupt the downward trend despite the presence of a white candle.

Composition:

1) During a series of trading session with persistently falling prices (bear markets), a relatively large black candle is created.

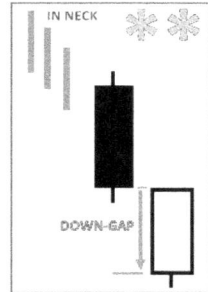

2) The following trading session opens with a DOWN GAP (windows down). During the trading session, the price rises to the level of the closing price of the previous black candle. The closing price is identical in both candles.

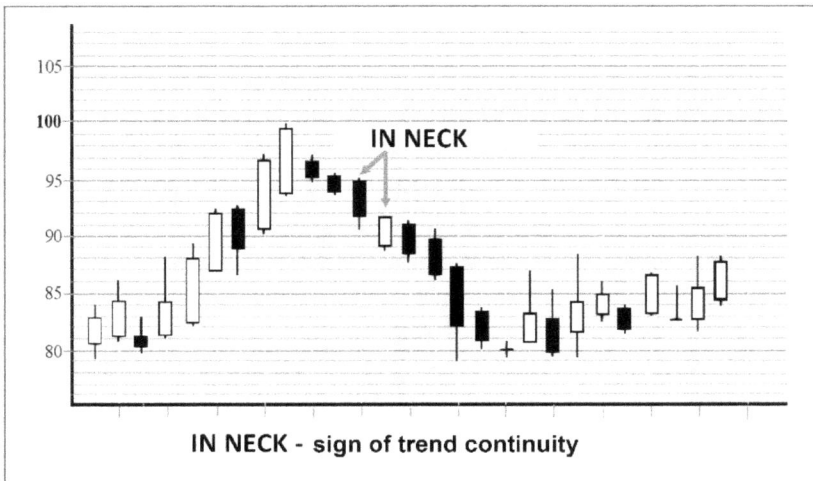

IN NECK - sign of trend continuity

Important: The white candle has no upper shadow!

No position is acquired without confirmation in the presence of a black candle in the following trading session.

The IN NECK must not be confused with the BULLISH MEETING LINE.

ON NECK

Despite the presence of a white candle, this candle combination does not interrupt the downward trend.

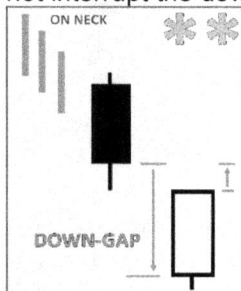

Composition:

1) During a series of trading sessions with persistently falling prices (bear markets), a relatively large black candle is created.

2) The following trading session opens with an impressive DOWN GAP (windows down). During the trading session, the price rises to the vicinity of the closing price of the previous black candle. The closing price of the white candle, at the same time highest reached price in the trading session, is below the closing price of the black candle.

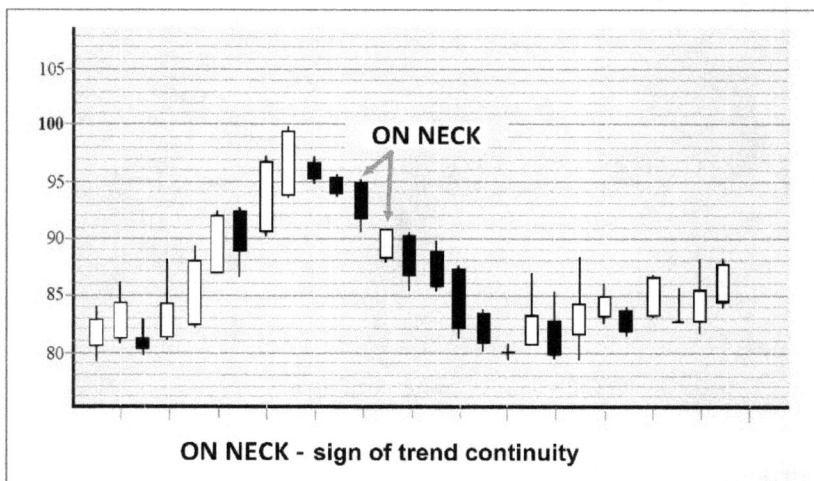

ON NECK - sign of trend continuity

No position is acquired without confirmation in the presence of a black candle in the following trading session.

The ON NECK must not be confused with the BULLISH MEETING LINE.

MEETING LINE BULLISH

This configuration is a sign of change in trend.

Composition:

1) At the end of a series of trading sessions with persistent falling prices (bear markets), a relatively great black candle is created.

2) The following trading session opens with an impressive DOWN GAP (windows down). The size of the DOWN-GAP must present a size at least 60% of the previous black candles' body. During the trading session, the price rises to the vicinity of the closing price of the previous black candle.

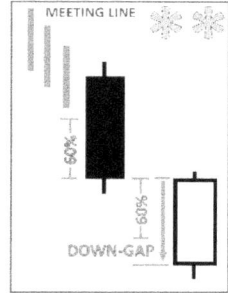

Market logic: After a sustained period of declining rates, a sufficient number of purchase requests reach the stop of the downward path.

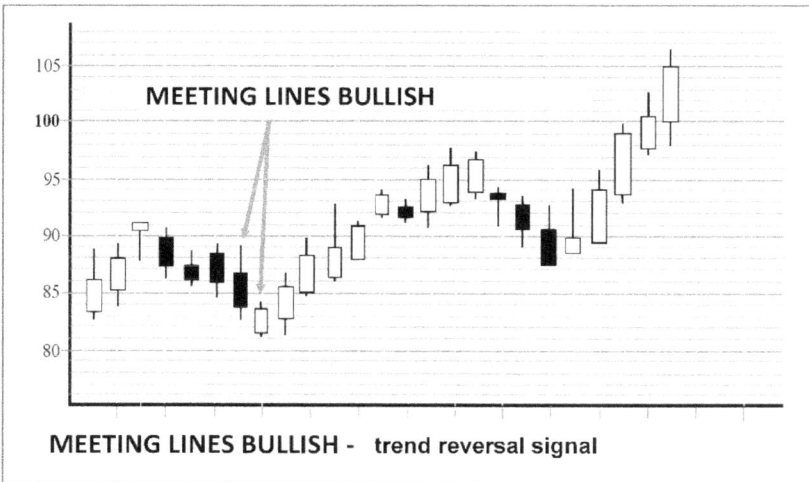

MEETING LINES BULLISH

MEETING LINES BULLISH - trend reversal signal

The sign of reversal trend is relatively weak. Therefore, the next trading sessions must bring the confirmation for an eventually position acquisition.

ENGULFING BULLISH

ENGULFING BULLISH

This candle combination is a strong sign of the trend change and is relatively often found in candle graphics.

Composition:

1) At the end of a long-running downward trend presents a relatively small black candle.

2) The second trading session opens with a DOWN GAP and a price that is positioned below the lower shadow of the black candle. During the trading session, the price goes far beyond the previous black candle including the upper shadow. At end of trading session, the graphic presents an overly large white candle, which completely covers the previous black candle including the two shadows.

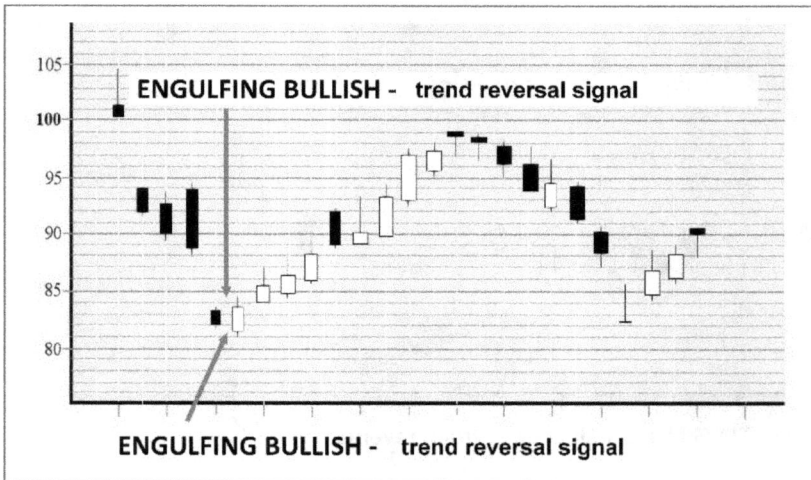
ENGULFING BULLISH - trend reversal signal

If the black candle is completely covered by the white candle, this candle combination is a very reliable sign of a trend reversal to rise, the uptrend.

UNIQUE THREE RIVER BOTTOM

The UNIQUE THREE RIVER BOTTOM is a configuration that announces end of the downtrend.

Composition:
1) At the end of a long series of downward trend, it presents a large black candle.

2) The following trading session begins with an UPWARD-GAP, which posts easily the opening price below the opening price of the previous session. The trading session produces a BLACK HAMMER.

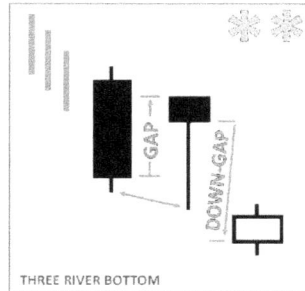

THREE RIVER BOTTOM

3) The third trading session begins with a DOWN GAP (windows down) and forms a small white candle.

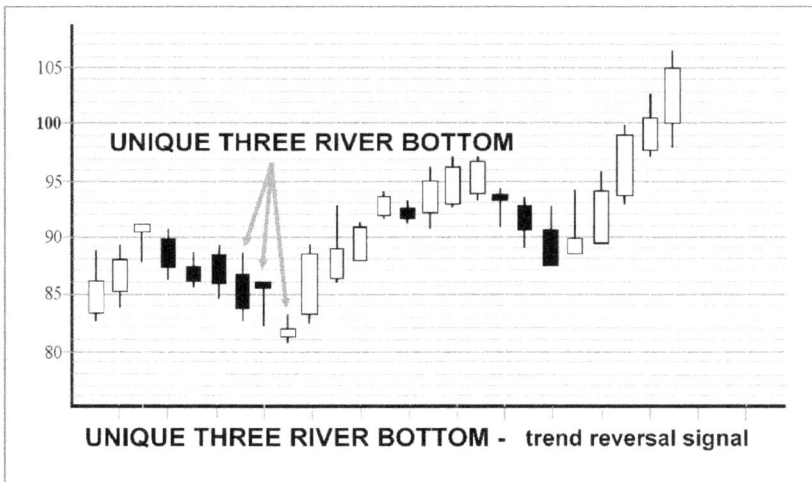

UNIQUE THREE RIVER BOTTOM

UNIQUE THREE RIVER BOTTOM - trend reversal signal

To reinforce significance of the reversal trend sign, the opening price of the WHITE SPINNING TOP must be lower than the lowest price of the previous candle . In the graph, the small white candle body is located with a DOWN GAP below the upper shadow of the previous HAMMER.

DOWNSIDE TASUKI GAP

This candle combination signals the continuation of the downward trend despite the presence of a white candle.

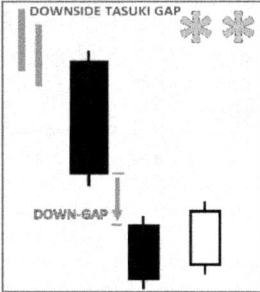

Configuration:

1) In a downtrend appears a large black candle.

2) The second trading session begins with a DOWN GAP, (windows down) and the price reduction continues. This session closes finally with a black candle with small shadows.

3) The third trading session presents a pseudo-inversion of the trend and is characterized by a white candle positioned due a small UPWARD-GAP. The inaugural price is situated inside the previous black candle body.

Important: Neither the body of the white candle, nor its upper shadow, may close the DOWN-GAP between the two BLACK candles.

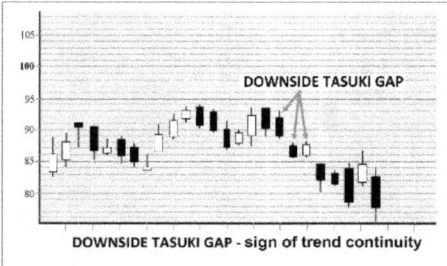

DOWNSIDE TASUKI GAP - sign of trend continuity

To confirm the continuation of the downward trend, the succeeding trading session of this DOWN SIDE TASUKI GAP should open below the closing price of the white candle without closing the GAP. This Gap was found between the black candle of the second trading session and the white candle.

DOWNSIDE GAP THREE METHODS

Despite the presence of a white candle, this candle constellation shall be regarded as a sign of continuity.

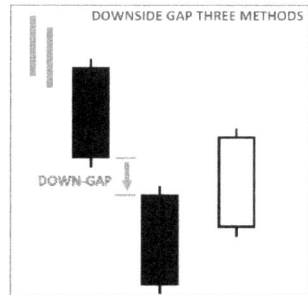

DOWNSIDE GAP THREE METHODS

DOWN-GAP

Composition:

1) The DOWN SIDE GAP THREE METHODS always begins next to the downward trend with an impressive price drop in the first trading session.

2) The second trading session opens with a DOWN GAP (windows down), and creates an equally large black candle compared to the previous candle.

3) The third trading session is dominated by a consolidation. The opening price is inside the first black candle body without penetrating much in the black candle's body. The result is a white candle that closes the DOWN GAP opened between previous two black candles.

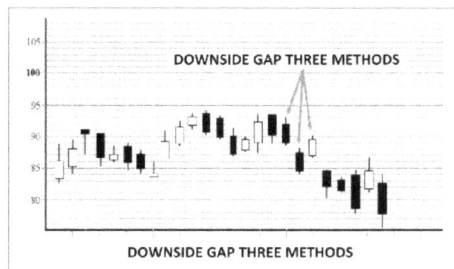

The DOWN SIDE GAP THREE METHOD necessarily requires confirmation in the following trading sessions.

DOWNSIDE GAP THREE METHODS

DOWNSIDE GAP THREE METHODS

The trend prediction of this candle combination is not particularly reliable. Many are the traders who see this figure as a sign of impending trend change instead of a sign of continuity.

SIXTH CHAPTER - #6

TREND: up or downward
LAST CANDLE: DOJI

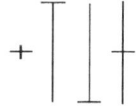

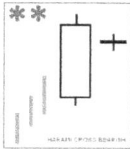
HARAMI CROSS BEARISH

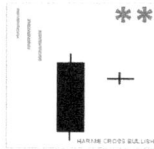
HARAMI CROSS BULLISH

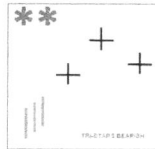
TRI-STARS BEARISH

TRI-STARS BULLISH

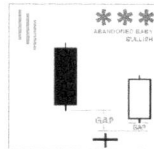
ABANDONED BABY BULLISH
GAP

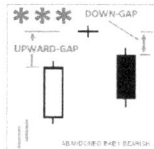
DOWN-GAP
UPWARD-GAP
ABANDONED BABY BEARISH

HARAMI CROSS BEARISH

The HARAMI CROSS BEARISH at the end of a longer-lasting upward trend is a reversal sign.

Market logic: After a large number of trading sessions in an uptrend, many market players hold the moment appropriate to think of a profit-taking. The buying demands decreases whereas the sale offers increases.

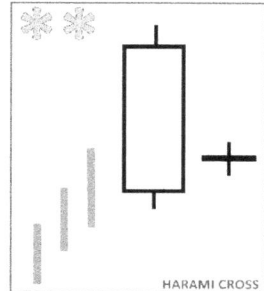

HARAMI CROSS

The significance of a reversible sign is stronger if

1. the deeper the DOJI, the second candle is placed in the lower part of the previous white candle,

2. and the white candle body is large enough to enclose the DOJI including its shadows.

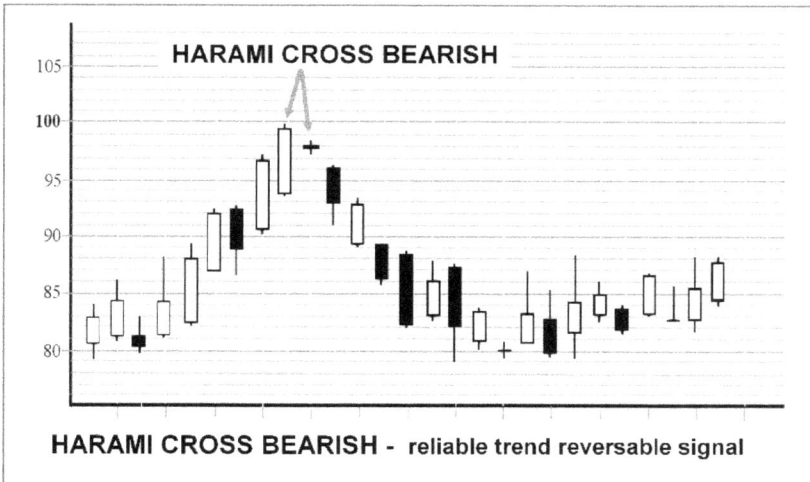

HARAMI CROSS BEARISH

HARAMI CROSS BEARISH - reliable trend reversable signal

The HARAMI CROSS BEARISH is regarded as a strong reversal sign.

HARAMI CROSS BULLISH

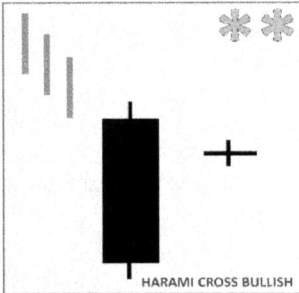

The HARAMI CROSS BULLISH at the end of a longer-lasting downtrend is a turning sign of ascendance.

Market logic: After an extended period in the downward trend, the price is considered to be undervalued. Sudden market dynamics allows the purchase to raise sharply. This in turn causes an immediate trend reversal.

HARAMI CROSS BULLISH

The significance of a reversible sign is stronger if

1. the higher the DOJI, the second candle is placed in the upper part of the previous black candle,
2. and the first black candle body is large enough to enclose the DOJI including its shadows.

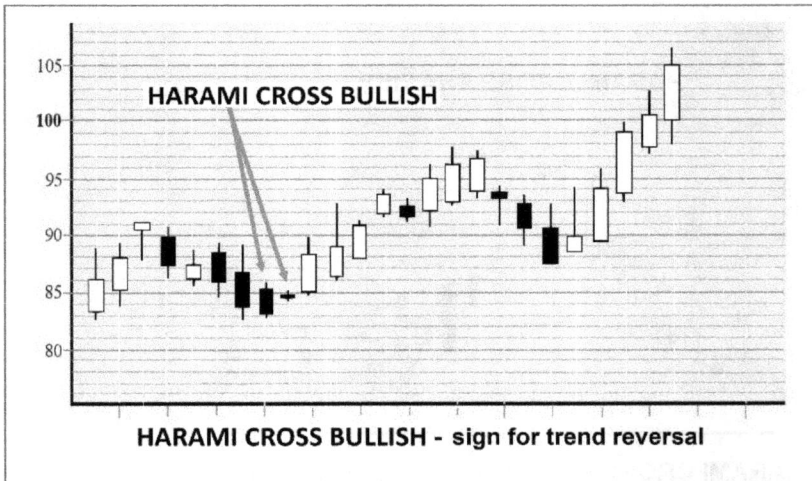

HARAMI CROSS BULLISH

HARAMI CROSS BULLISH - sign for trend reversal

The HARAMI CROSS BULLISH is considered as a relatively reliable reversal sign.

BEARISH TRI-STAR

The BEARISH TRI-STAR at the end of a longer-lasting uptrend is considered as a trend reversal sign.

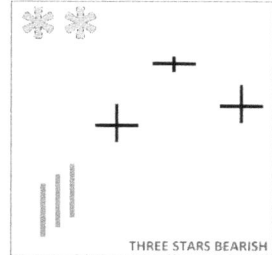

THREE STARS BEARISH

Market logic: If a Doji alone is sufficient to express the uncertainty of the market operators, so this mood amplified many times when three Dojis appear in the graph.

Composition:
1) In the first trading session, a DOJI appears in an UPWARD-GAP.

2) The second trading session opens also with a significant UPWARD-GAP. The candle of this second trading session is also a DOJI with very little shadows.

3) The third trading session begins with a DOWN-GAP, and places a third DOJI.

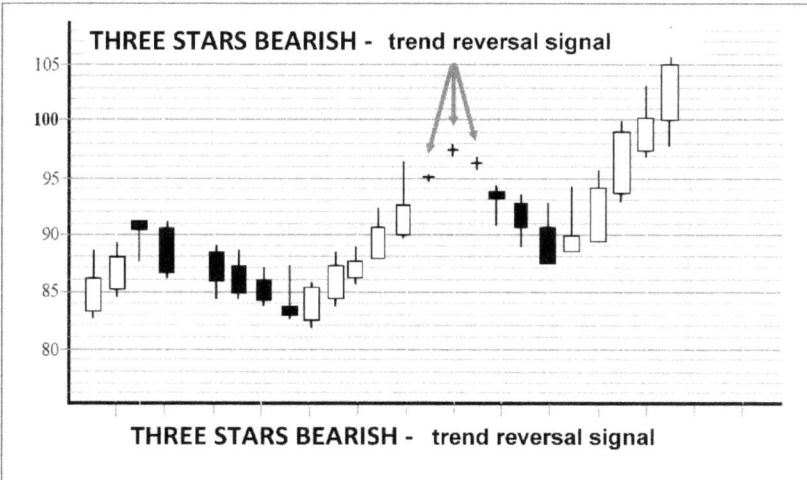

THREE STARS BEARISH - trend reversal signal

This candle configuration is seen very rarely. However, it is likely a reversal trend sign.

BULLISH TRI-STAR

THREE STARS BULLISH

The BULLISH TRI-STAR at the end of a longer-lasting downtrend often signals a reversal trend.

Market logic: If a Doji alone is sufficient to express the uncertainty of the market operators, so this mood amplified many times when three Dojis appear in the graph.

Composition:

1) In the first trading session, a DOJI appears in a DOWNWARD-GAP.
2) The second trading session opens also with a significant DOWN GAP. The candle of this second trading session is also a DOJI with very little shadows.
3) The third trading session begins with an UPWARD-GAP, and places a third DOJI.

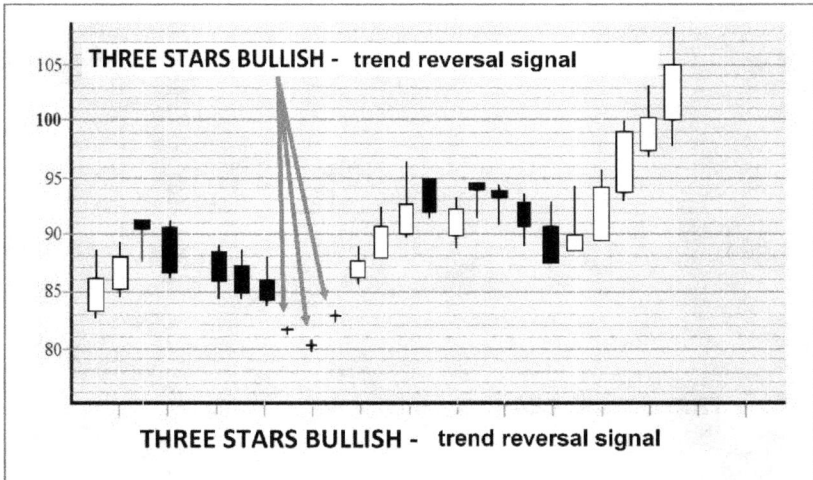

THREE STARS BULLISH - trend reversal signal

THREE STARS BULLISH - trend reversal signal

This candle configuration is very rare. However, it is likely a reversal sign for future bullish trend.

ABANDONED BABY BULLISH

This candle combination at the end of a longer-lasting downtrend often signals a trend reversal.

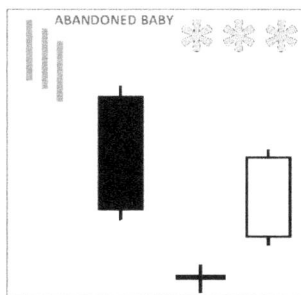

Composition:

1) In the first trading session, a large black candle testifies the interest of market players through mass sales continuing to push the price.

2) The second trading session opens with a significant DOWN GAP. The candle body is a DOJI with little shadows.

3) The third trading session begins with an UPWARD-GAP. During this trading session, the price goes up massively to penetrate a maximum in the black candle's body of the first trading session.

In this candle combination the shadows play an important role.

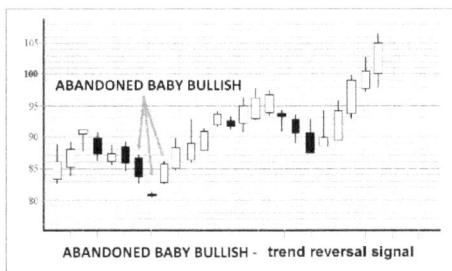

ABANDONED BABY BULLISH - trend reversal signal

No contact may occur between the lower shadow of the first black candle, the lower shadow of white candle and the upper shadow of the DOJI.

This is the reason of the name "Lost Baby".

ABANDONED BABY BEARISH

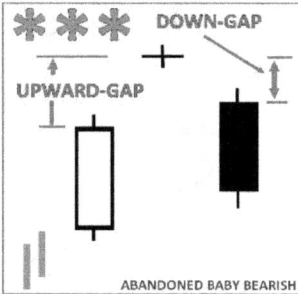

ABANDONED BABY BEARISH

The ABANDONED BABY BEARISH at the end of a longer-lasting upward trend often signals a trend reversal.

Composition:

1) In the first trading session, a large white candle testifies the presence of a strong buying interest.

2) The second trading session opens with a significant UPWARD-GAP. The candle is a DOJI with little upper and lower shadows. It expresses the indecision of the market operators.

3) The third trading session begins with a DOWN GAP. During this trading session, the price falls massively into the body of the first trading session and penetrates a maximum into the white candle's body.

ABANDONED BABY BEARISH - trend reversal signal

Even in this candle combination the shadows play an important role.

There may be no contact between the upper shadow of the first white candle, the upper shadow of the black candle and the lower shadow of DOJI.

No contact between all three candles and their shadows is the reason of the name "Lost Baby".

ANNEX

EFFICIENCY of candles analysis

The PER - price-earnings ratio

VOLUME – value trading session sales

The RSI - relative strength indicator

EFFICIENCY OF CANDLE CHARTS

The Japanese candlestick charts used to predict price changes are infallible tools. They can be both excellent to send signs that can be followed, but they can also produce false signals.

The efficiency of a candle prediction depends mainly on the quality of the underlying asset. The base value can be a stock, a bond, a derivative, cash, a raw material or any other exchange traded product.

Before any investment project, the market operators should first look the underlying asset under the microscope. It is not enough to look at the current situation. The behavior of the underlying asset should be inspected over a longer period. That is, the market player should be satisfied not only with the consideration of a technical chart but he should also procure sufficient basic information about the underlying asset. If this information is mediocre or even be regarded as bad, so the candle predictions should find no means as an observance.

Generally speaking, the solidity of these underlying assets are as secure as the predictions of candlestick charts! It shows: Candles which treat seriously the market-values should be followed; less secured values should not be followed.

But even if the underlying asset can be considered as good or even very good, the market player should always consult a second or even third chart support or an additional technical indicator before he takes to decide a position.

VOLUME - TRADING SESSION SALES

No professional trader, no private investors who thinks logical about the risks of his capital investments because he received only a single hint of buying or selling at whatever type of sign - technical analysis or commercial information . Who would have the courage to put his capital at risk? Just because in the market corridors, a rumor passes by that this or that stock would perform a miracle?

A candlestick chart sign should receive a confirmation. This can be done by a longer viewing of the candle's figures and their results in the following trading sessions or another additional help criterion outside of candlesticks. The candlesticks win their value only by applying with caution.

Among the variety of possibilities of confirmations, two offers particularly at:

1. The most immediate available information about the acquired paper is the PRICE-EARNING RATIOS, shortly called PER ;

2. the number or the generated sales of traded papers in the last trading session.

These two information, when combined if possible, yet offers no warranty. However, they increase the level of security of an imminent investment decision by multiple.

What incurs in a trading session on SALES VOLUME is an information-rich market indicator. It provides information on activity and sales and is an excellent barometer of the current mood of the market operators.

Example:

If only few papers were implemented, a signal sent from the candle analysis is to be regarded only as a WEAK SIGNAL.

However if sales were significant, so the candle signal is also gaining importance.

Other example:

If the sales decrease regularly, so the stock market traders can expect an approaching termination of the current trends and treats this position with respect.

The same applies to a permanent increase of sales; a change of trend is expected.

The VOLUME of sales provides a wide range of reliable information. These two examples are intended to illustrate only the advantage in case sellers or buyers have knowledge of volume of sales.

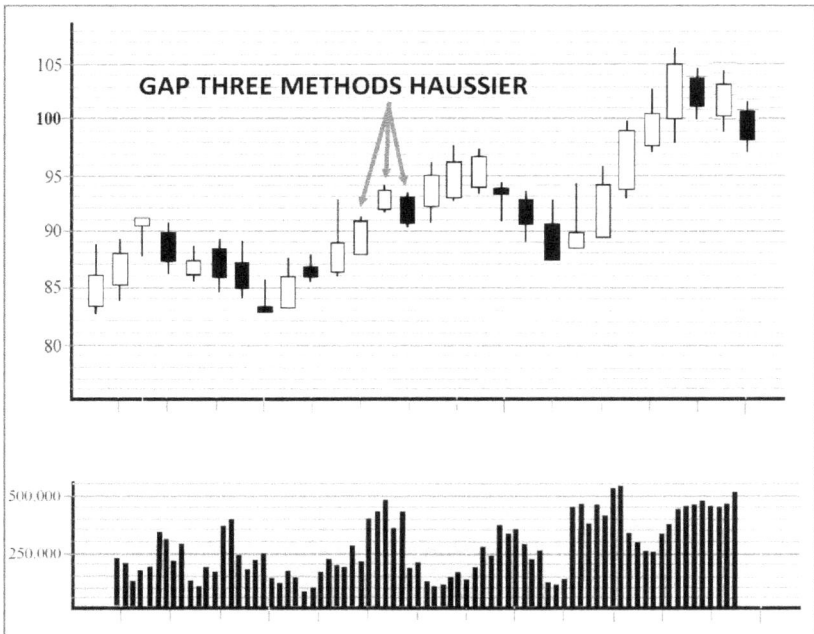

GAP THREE METHODS HAUSSIER

In the graphics, SALES VOLUME is displayed mostly with vertical bars below the corresponding candles charts.

Price Earnings Ratio (PER)

One of the most commonly used evaluation criteria for trade exchange companies is the price-earnings ratio, abbreviated as PER. Although this PER leaves many factors of stock exchange ignored, it informs the stockbrokers on the simple manner to arrive on the expected return of its investment.

The PER is calculated by dividing the stock PRICE by the distributed PROFITS of the stock, (this PROFIT is called distributed DIVIDEND).

The formula:

PER = share price / earnings per share.

Generally, the numbers of the last annual balance sheet or the last quarterly report are the ones used to calculate the PER. However, traders and financial analysts with insider knowledge often uses projected figures during ongoing operations.

Example:

- The current price of a share is 34 $.
- The distributed profit for the year amounted to $ 4 per share.
- Dividing the share price, that's 34 by dividend 4 (profit), the result is 8.5.
- The PER (price-earnings ratio), in this example is 8.5.

In other words, the investor would have to wait 8½ years to get its costs of shares purchased back.
This results in the sense of the COST-INCOME RATIO: The smaller the PER, the cheaper is the current price of a stock.

Example:
Date: 13/08/2012 Industry: Petrochemicals

- ESSO   rate 57.20 $ PER = 11.88,
- MAUREL ÖL   rate 12.94 $ PER = 8.56,
- TOTAL GABON   rate 339.85 $ PER = 6.84,
- TOTAL   rate 39.88 $ PER = 6.64.

Conclusion: provided a uniform corporate development in the oil sector, the stock ESSO is overrated, too expensive, and the price of the stock TOTAL is extremely well priced.

Or in other words: With uniform corporate development without free distribution of bonus shares or the unexpected discovery of an unknown new oil field, the investor needs 11 years and 10 months to recoup his money from his ESSO investment, whereas 6 years and 7 months are sufficient to obtain the money back from his TOTAL investment.

Of course, this comparison method can be applied only inside a corporate sector. It would be total nonsense, to compare the PER of a hypermarket chain with the PER of an industrial company.

If the PRICE-EARNING RATIOS from industrial companies is relatively low (normal average values are between 7.5 to 12.5), shares of trading companies usually are rated significantly higher (normal average values are between 9.0 and 22.5). The cause of this unequal reviews lies in the different industry profit expectations on the part of the market players.

It is also noted that the PER bill emanates not only from the constant and steady dividend payment over the years, but also from a uniform, almost linear corporate development. Unfortunately, this is rarely the case. This is one of the reasons why the PER cannot be a sole buy or sell sign. But it can be a suitable additional indication from a candlestick signal.

The PRICE-EARNING RATIOS, if interpreted correctly even in exceptional situations, makes possible the early detection of speculative market interventions. A PER to dizzying heights far beyond the customary range is feared to form that so called "stock market bubble", which advises extreme caution. Over the past, such "stock market bubbles" have caused significant damage. Many small investors could have never recover their losses.

R S I - Relative Strength Index

A highly successful accompanying indicator of candlesticks especially for long-term investment position is the RSI, the Relative Strength Indicator.

The RSI is an average indicator and is concerned with the upward or downward movement of the converted title or share. It answers the question on whether in a given period of upward or downward trend of a paper is in the majority. It indicates whether in a past period,(for example, 7, 9, 14 or 21 days), there were more sales deals or more purchase requests.

As already said several times, the trading exchange often develops independent action energy. That is, if a paper finds in particular a strong interest, so the market develops a synergy that increases the volume traded in actual disproportionately.

In other words, once a paper with several stockbrokers takes attention and is traded, other traders hook up to this trend. And without this, is a market-appropriate basis for their actions. This phenomenon or this synergy increases automatically the more stockbrokers are interested in a traded paper.

A large purchase demand increases the price - a large sell supply decreases the price.

This can lead to interesting extremes. If a paper reacted significantly below their intrinsic or fair value, it is called an "oversold paper". If a paper sells much against its inner or fair value, it is called an "overbought paper".

The "intrinsic value" of a paper corresponding to that in a fundamental value analysis of the basic value, a "fair" price emerged in the underlying company or the related real estate.

The RSI is based on the average price changes within a time period; in which the upward movements with the downward movements are compared.

To calculate the RSI, the graphic designer first selects a time period..

For example: RSI-7 for a period of 7 days, RSI-14 for 14 days or RSI 21 for 21 days. A few moments of trading RSI, (i.e RSI-7 or RSI-9), is suitable for DAY-TRADING, while an RSI-21, thus expressing 21 trading days, proved particularly in LONG-TERM INVESTMENTS.

The RSI is represented graphically as follows:

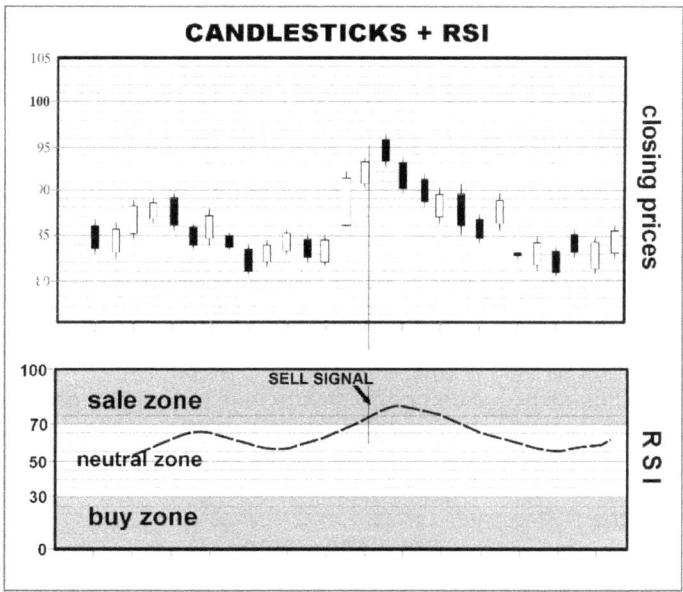

CANDLESTICKS + RSI

Such graphic illustrates value and usefulness of RSI:

Rising the RSI in the sales area, (rises above 70 in this figure), the paper can be considered "overbought". In this case, the indicator can be viewed in conjunction with a sign of candles analysis as sufficiently secured selling sign.

Falling the RSI however in the purchase zone, (falls below 30 in the graph), the paper can be considered "oversold". In this case, the indicator can be viewed in conjunction with a sign of candles analysis as sufficiently secured buying sign.

The mathematical calculation of the RSI is as follows:

$$RSI = 100 - [100 / (1+y)]$$

The result of this formula is always a value between 0 and 100.

The letter Y represents the result of dividing the average upward movements by the average downward movements.

An example to better understand to this formula:

7 market quotations: 75, 73, 75, 77, 75, 80 and 76:

1. Market quotation = 75
2. Market quotation = 73 that is -2 to previous quotation
3. Market quotation = 75 that is +2 to previous quotation
4. Market quotation = 77 that is +2 to previous quotation
5. Market quotation = 74 that is -3 to previous quotation
6. Market quotation = 79 that is +5 to previous quotation
7. Market quotation = 75 that is -4 to previous quotation.

If one now adds all plus points, this gives 9 plus points;
If one now adds all negative points, this results in 9 minus points.
Coincidentally, in these 7 quotations has given 9 points up and 9 points down.

In memory, the RSI formula is:
$$RSI = 100 - [100 / (1+y)]$$
To determine the unknown variable Y, first the plus points, (so in this example 9), are divided by the number of quotations, (so 7), and one receives the result of 1.29. Then the minus points, (so in this example 9), divided by the number of quotations, (so 7), and one receives also the result of 1.29.

y = 1.29 divided by 1.29 = 1

Repeat the RSI formula:
RSI = 100 − [100 / (1+y)]
RSI = 100 − [100 / (1 + 1,29/1,29)]
RSI = 100 − [100 / (1 + 1)]
RSI = 100 − [100 / 2]
RSI = 100 − 50
# Result: RSI = 50

This means that the previous 7 quotations give an RSI of 50 points.

Thus, the RSI is positioned exactly in the middle of the NEUTRAL ZONE. This neutrality area at 50 points signals around a balance between purchase requests and offers to sell, and thus the balance between buyers and sellers.

Simplified, it can be said about the RSI that it can be in conjunction with the information from a candlestick chart, a fairly reliable help to acquire a position.

Bibliography

"Encyclopedia of Candlestick Charts" by Thomas N. Bulkowski
editor: Wiley – 2009 ;

"Candlestick Charting Demystified" by Wayne A. Corbitt
editor: McGraw-Hill – 2012
ISBN-13 : 978-0071799874 ;

"Candlestick Charting Explained" by Gregory L. Morris
editor: McGraw-Hill – 1992
ISBN-13 : 978-1557388919;

"Candlestick Charting for Dummies" by Russell Rhoads
editor: John Wiley & Sons Ltd –2008
ISBN-13 : 978-0470178089 ;

"Candlestick-Charttechnik" by Thomas Gebert and Paul Hüsgen
editor: Börsenbuchverlag – 2004
ISBN-13 : 978-3922669579 ;

"Technische Aktienanalyse" by Christian Schroder
editor: Grin – 2007 - ISBN-13 : 978-3638651066 ;

"Les Chandeliers Japonais" – Introduction & guide premiers pas –
Editor: Bod- Books on Demand – 2012
ISBN 13: 978-2-81061313106

"Les chandeliers Japonais, un guide contemporain sur d'anciennes
techniques d'investissement venues d'Extrême-Orient" by Steve Nison
– editor: Valor – 1999 - ISBN-13 : 978-2909356082 ;

"Chandeliers japonais : Figures d'indécision et de continuation" by
François Baron – editor : Eyrolles – 2010
ISBN-13 : 978-2212547238 ;

"Maitriser l'analyse technique avec Thami Kabbaj : 10 leçons pour
gagner" – by Thami Kabbaj – editor: Eyrolles - 2011
ISBN-13 : 978-2212549560 ;

INTERNET - HOMEPAGES

www.tradingview.com

www.thestreet.com

www. candlecharts.com

www.investopedia.com

www.boersen-lexikon.com

www.tradingbrothers.com

www.investor-verlag.de

www.boersenjunkies.de

www.boersennews.de

www.boersenuni.com

www.trading212.com

www.faz.net

www.kapitaleinkommen.de

www.charttec.de

www.americanbuls.com

www.finanznachrichten.de

www.trading-school.eu

About the collaborator,

Iskia Diane Salatan,

she hails from the Philippines.

She also has experience in English tutorial and has already extended assistance in editing and proofreading jobs. Proper instruction and establishing good communication can contribute to the success of any endeavor.

For assistance, you may contact her thru:

Iskia.Salatan@gmail.com

www.ingramcontent.com/pod-product-compliance
Lightning Source LLC
Chambersburg PA
CBHW060042210326

41520CB00009B/1238